P9-BYR-687

A Child's First Library of Learning

How Things Work

TIME-LIFE BOOKS • ALEXANDRIA, VIRGINIA

Contents

Why Does a Rubber Ball Bounce?

(ANSWER) When a rubber ball hits a hard surface it flattens the rubber and squeezes the air inside the ball. Then the air inside tries to push the rubber back to its original shape. The force of the air is what makes a ball bounce.

How a ball bounces

■ **When it's full of air**

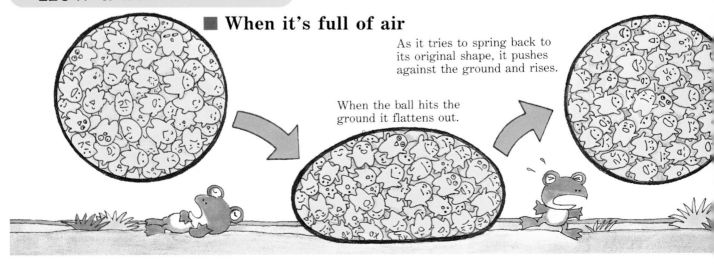

As it tries to spring back to its original shape, it pushes against the ground and rises.

When the ball hits the ground it flattens out.

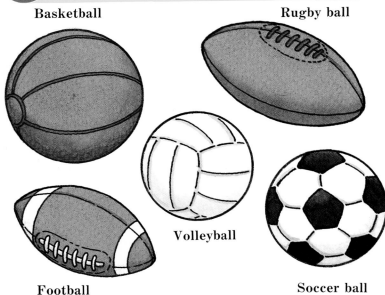

Basketball   Rugby ball

Volleyball

Football   Soccer ball

Many sports are played with balls which are filled with air to make them bounce better. For most sports, balls are round, but not for football or Rugby. These sports have balls that look a lot alike. How many of the different sports here have you played? Can you think of any other popular games that are played with a rubber ball filled with air?

■ When there isn't enough air

If the ball isn't completely full of air it doesn't have much power to push back against the ground, so it doesn't bounce very well.

● To the Parent

The tendency of an object or substance to return to its original size and shape after being changed by outside pressure is called elasticity. In a rubber ball the rubber itself has some elasticity, although the pressure of the inside air is largely responsible for making the ball bounce. Children who have had the experience of trying to bounce a ball that has lost some of its air should know that. They may also realize that a rubber ball will naturally lose some of its air over a period of time.

Why Do Balloons Rise Into the Sky?

ANSWER Some balloons are filled with an extra-light gas called helium. It makes the balloons lighter than the air around them, so they float upward.

The rubber that a balloon is made of has holes in it that are so tiny you can't see them. But those tiny holes let the gas in the balloon leak out little by little, and after a while the balloon is deflated. Balloons that had helium in them sink to the ground.

The balloon is filled with helium gas from a tank, and then the mouth of the balloon is sealed.

■ Which is lighter?

A balloon that has been filled with helium gas

A balloon you've blown up by mouth

■ But it's still lighter than water

Even regular air is lighter than water, so a beach ball will pop back up to the surface quickly if you push it under the water.

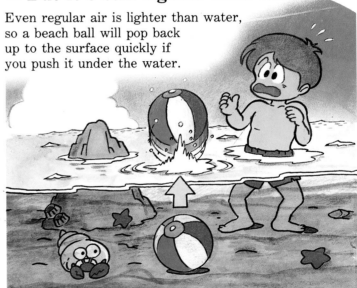

● To the Parent

Hydrogen is the lightest gas in the atmosphere. It is not usually used to inflate balloons, however, because it is highly inflammable. Helium, although not as light as hydrogen, is seven times lighter than air and is safe because it is not inflammable. A helium-filled balloon released in a room at first will rise to the ceiling and stay there. With gas leaking slowly through pores in the rubber, the balloon's buoyancy in the air decreases enough to be balanced by its weight, so it drifts downward and floats around the room.

❓ Why Does a Yo-Yo Go Up and Down?

ANSWER A yo-yo starts moving downward because of its own weight. As it turns it starts to unwind some of the string wrapped around its center. At the end of the string the yo-yo keeps turning, so it starts rewinding the string. As the string rewinds it pulls the yo-yo upward. And if you pull on the string it helps the yo-yo move upward to your hand.

Simple yo-yo

The string is attached to the center shaft.

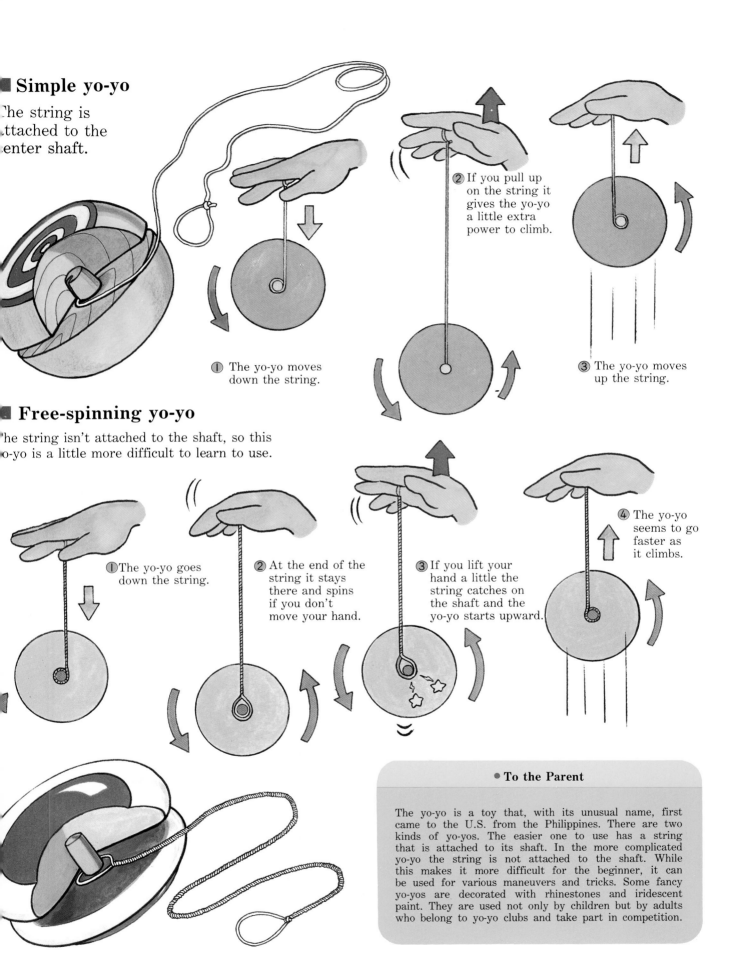

① The yo-yo moves down the string.

② If you pull up on the string it gives the yo-yo a little extra power to climb.

③ The yo-yo moves up the string.

Free-spinning yo-yo

The string isn't attached to the shaft, so this yo-yo is a little more difficult to learn to use.

① The yo-yo goes down the string.

② At the end of the string it stays there and spins if you don't move your hand.

③ If you lift your hand a little the string catches on the shaft and the yo-yo starts upward.

④ The yo-yo seems to go faster as it climbs.

• To the Parent

The yo-yo is a toy that, with its unusual name, first came to the U.S. from the Philippines. There are two kinds of yo-yos. The easier one to use has a string that is attached to its shaft. In the more complicated yo-yo the string is not attached to the shaft. While this makes it more difficult for the beginner, it can be used for various maneuvers and tricks. Some fancy yo-yos are decorated with rhinestones and iridescent paint. They are used not only by children but by adults who belong to yo-yo clubs and take part in competition.

❓ Why Does a Top Spin?

ANSWER Once they start, some things will keep on spinning for a while. Tops do this because of their shape. They spin for a long time before they finally slow down and stop.

TRY THIS

Take a piece of cardboard and cut out different shapes like those you see here. Put a sharpened pencil through them and see which ones make the best tops when you spin them. What will happen when you move the piece of cardboard up or down on the pencil? Try it.

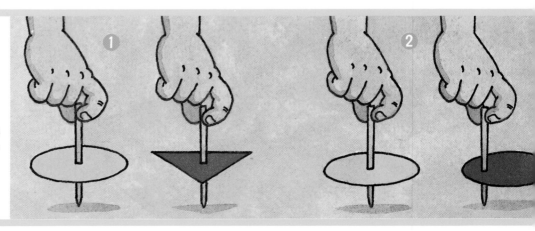

10

Wind a string around the top and pull it hard to set the top spinning.

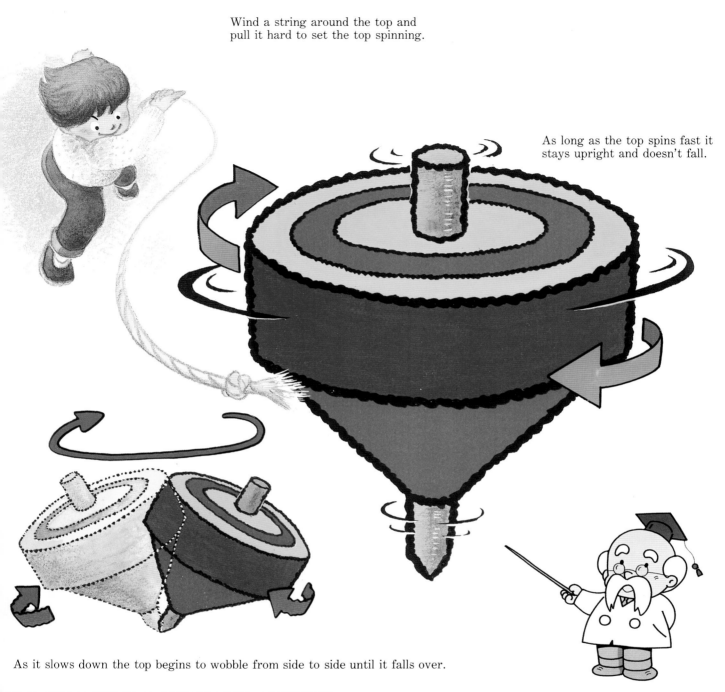

As long as the top spins fast it stays upright and doesn't fall.

As it slows down the top begins to wobble from side to side until it falls over.

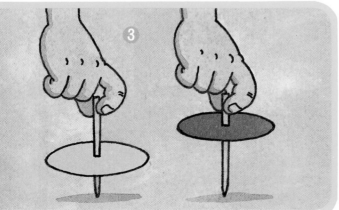

● **To the Parent**

For many centuries and in many cultures, tops have amused children and adults alike. With practice it is possible to make a top move along a string or balance on a very small point. Other objects such as coins can also be made to spin fast and stay upright for a while. Objects tend to keep spinning because of the law of inertia. Being heavy, rotating at high speed and having a completely symmetrical shape are the factors that keep a top spinning. As the top spins at high speed it is stable. When its speed of rotation decreases it begins to lean to one side and then to the other under the influence of gravity. As the top slows down more it begins to wobble, then eventually falls over and stops.

⍰ Why Does a Pinwheel Turn?

ANSWER A pinwheel turns when the wind pushes against its blades. The shape of the blades makes it easy for them to catch the wind. You can see how the wind blows against the blades and makes the pinwheel spin faster and faster.

■ **How the wind makes a pinwheel turn**

■ A variety of pinwheels

■ Members of the family

▲ **Windmill**

The power of the wind makes the wheels of the windmill turn, and as the wheels turn they pump water or grind grain.

▲ **Wind-powered generator**

Electricity is generated when the wind turns the blades.

TRY THIS

■ Make a pinwheel

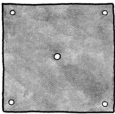

Make a hole in the center and at each corner of a square piece of paper.

Cut the paper as shown by the dotted lines here.

Gently place the corner holes over the center one.

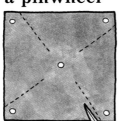

Put a shaft in the holes.

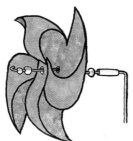

Attach the shaft to a handle.

• To the Parent

The pinwheel is a traditional toy found in many parts of the world. The force of the wind on its blades is what makes the pinwheel spin. Windmills and wind-powered generators of electricity use wind power in the same way. Windmills once were used in the Netherlands and other European countries to pump water and mill grain. They are still used to pump water in some parts of the U.S.

? Why Does a Balancing Toy Rock?

Give it a gentle push with your finger.

ANSWER The toy rocks because it's moving to a position where it will be perfectly in balance. When the toy is balanced the rocking stops.

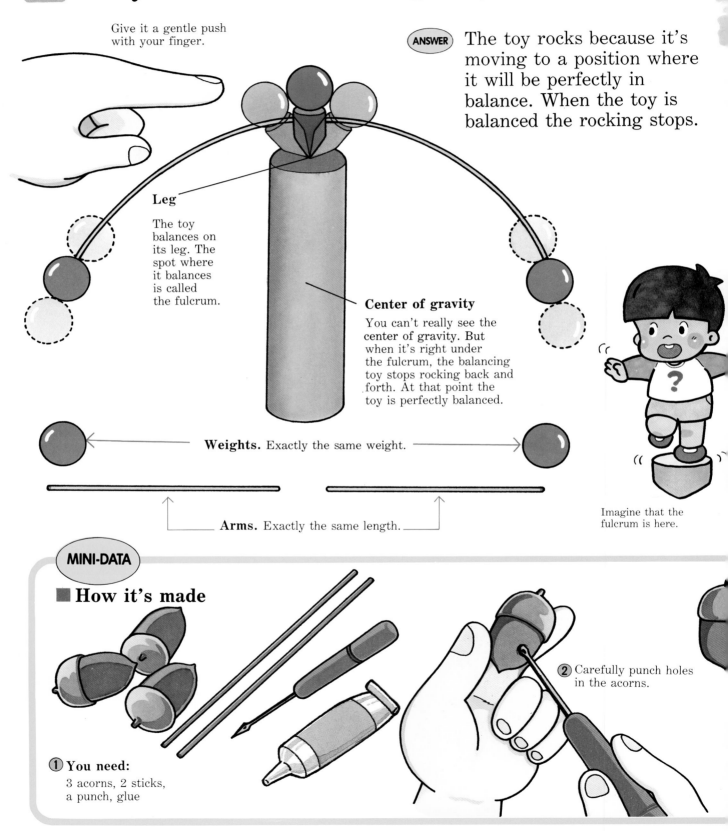

Leg

The toy balances on its leg. The spot where it balances is called the fulcrum.

Center of gravity

You can't really see the center of gravity. But when it's right under the fulcrum, the balancing toy stops rocking back and forth. At that point the toy is perfectly balanced.

Weights. Exactly the same weight.

Arms. Exactly the same length.

Imagine that the fulcrum is here.

MINI-DATA

■ **How it's made**

① **You need:**
3 acorns, 2 sticks, a punch, glue

② Carefully punch holes in the acorns.

Oh! Too far to one side!

Hey! Not so far over!

③ Insert the sticks into the holes in the acorns and glue them in. Be sure both sticks are the same length.

● To the Parent

If the toy is to balance, the center of gravity must be right under the fulcrum. The arms should extend below the center acorn, and both end acorns should have the same weight. If the arms do not weigh exactly the same, the toy will still balance but not as easily. The acorns can be replaced by other materials.

How Do Scissors Cut Things?

ANSWER Scissors have two blades. The blades are fastened together so that they fit tightly but can still move freely. When you use scissors to cut something, the two blades rub against each other. You can cut straight or curved lines with them.

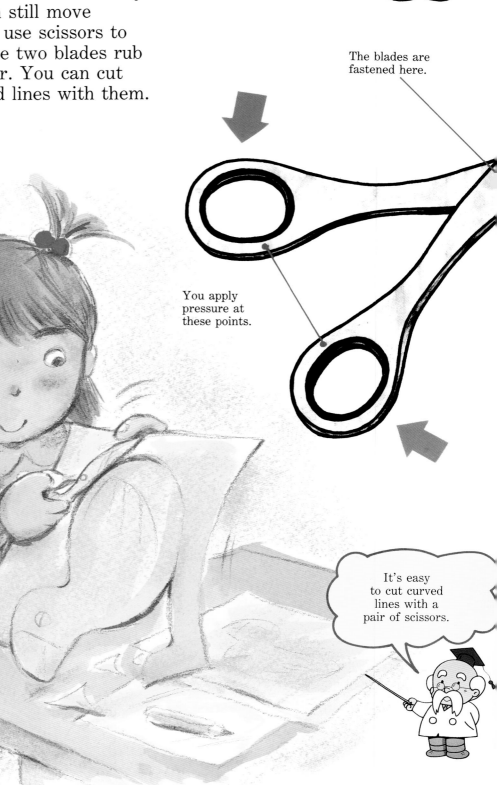

The blades are fastened here.

You apply pressure at these points.

It's easy to cut curved lines with a pair of scissors.

16

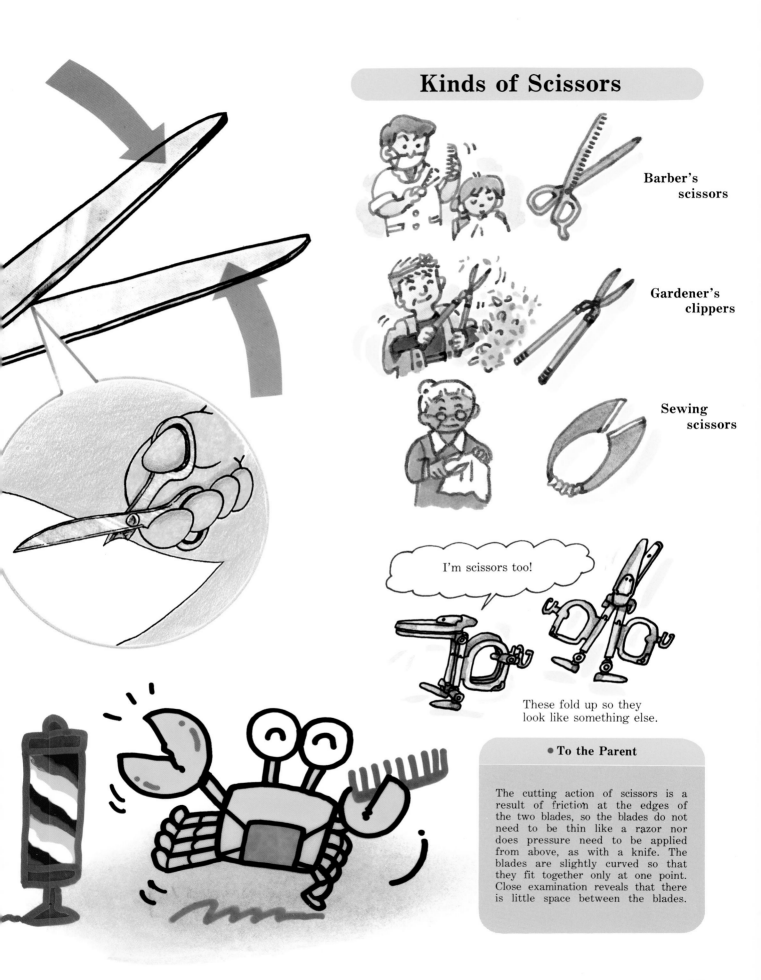

Kinds of Scissors

Barber's scissors

Gardener's clippers

Sewing scissors

I'm scissors too!

These fold up so they look like something else.

● **To the Parent**

The cutting action of scissors is a result of friction at the edges of the two blades, so the blades do not need to be thin like a razor nor does pressure need to be applied from above, as with a knife. The blades are slightly curved so that they fit together only at one point. Close examination reveals that there is little space between the blades.

How Does a Water Pistol Shoot Water?

ANSWER The hole where water comes out of a water pistol is very small. When water is forced through that hole, it comes squirting out with quite a lot of force.

MINI-DATA

■ **A simple water pistol**

Push in the plunger.

This large water pistol has only one chamber.

Don't push me!

Whew! We finally got out!

There's no place to go!

The plunger is made by wrapping cloth around a stick so that it fits tightly inside the chamber.

There's a small hole at the end.

How a Water Pump Works

When the handle of a pump is pulled up, the valve at the bottom opens and water is sucked into the pressure chamber.

If the handle is pushed down, the valve will close, and water will shoot out of the hose.

① Load the pistol with water.

② The red ball works the same way the valve does in the pump. When you pull the trigger water shoots through the hose and out of the pistol.

③ When you let the trigger go, more water is sucked in for the next time you shoot.

■ Which is better, a large or a small hole?

A small hole makes the water shoot farther than a large one does.

Small hole

Water goes a long way.

Large hole

Water doesn't go very far.

● To the Parent

The relationship between the size of the hole in a water pistol and the distance it can shoot water can be illustrated by spraying water out of a garden hose. If the nozzle is adjusted so that there is only a small opening at the end of the hose, the water shoots out farther. Because the volume of water does not change under pressure, a water pistol can use pressure to shoot water out. Now there are water pistols that are powered by batteries.

19

Why Do Fireworks Spread in the Sky?

ANSWER Fireworks use three kinds of gunpowder to make them work. Launching powder shoots fireworks into the sky. Expansion powder explodes and makes the fireworks spread. Finally star powder burns in different colors as the fireworks keep spreading through the sky.

■ How fireworks spread out

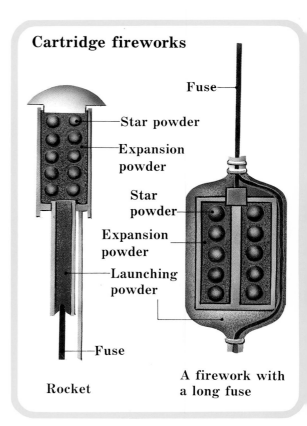

Outside the ball, the star powder burns and spreads out.

The expansion powder explodes. It spreads out the star powder.

The burning star powder then spreads out and changes colors.

■ Looking inside fireworks

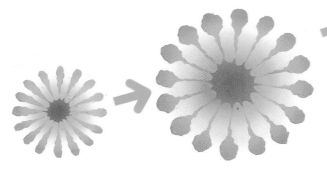

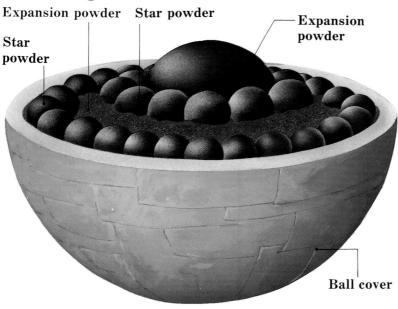

Expansion powder   Star powder

Star powder

Expansion powder

Ball cover

Cartridge fireworks

Fuse

Star powder

Expansion powder

Star powder

Expansion powder

Launching powder

Fuse

Rocket

A firework with a long fuse

▲ **Fire flowers.** In a dark sky, they really do spread out like a big flower.

 # Why Do Fireworks Have So Many Colors?

There are many colors in fireworks because various kinds of metal powder are mixed in with the star powder. Most metal powders make different colors when they burn. For example strontium makes a red flame, sodium a yellow one and barium a green one.

There are many kinds of fireworks. Each has colors of its own and spreads differently.

Gunpowder Strontium Gunpowder Sodium Gunpowder Barium

It burns red.   It burns yellow.   It burns green.

● **To the Parent**

Launched fireworks use launching powder to propel a lump of expansion powder and star powder into the sky. Black gunpowder (made from charcoal, niter and sulfur) once was used for fireworks, but it had a low burning temperature, and the color, orange, was not judged to be a good color. Potassium perchlorate is the powder most often used today. It produces much more heat, so that it can burn chemicals like strontium carbonate, which creates truly beautiful colors.

Why Do Things Appear to Be Backward in a Mirror?

ANSWER We see objects when light reflects off them. When we look at a mirror light reflects twice. It bounces off the object into the mirror and back to our eyes. Because of the way light travels, things appear backward.

■ Water is a mirror

The surface of quiet water is smooth, so it reflects images the way a mirror does.

When the wind blows it makes the surface rough, and the water can't reflect images.

TRY THIS

Look in a three-panel mirror like this one.

Kinds of Mirrors

▶ Curved mirror

This kind of mirror helps drivers see around a corner before they pull out into the street.

▼ Rear-view mirror

This mirror lets a driver see what's behind the car. It's slightly rounded so the driver can get a better view.

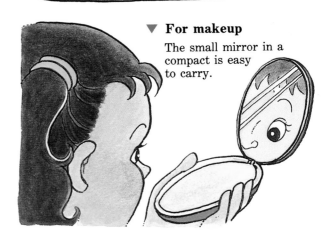

▼ For makeup

The small mirror in a compact is easy to carry.

● To the Parent

Children like to look at mirrors. Small children may turn a mirror over and look at the back as they try to understand how it works. An explanation of how a mirror reflects light probably will be difficult for a child to understand. It may be more instructive to use a small hand mirror simply to demonstrate the basic principles of light reflection. You can use it to reflect light, for instance, or set it on a book to show how the pages are reflected in reversed images.

How Does a Camera Take Pictures?

ANSWER A camera works much the way your eye does. When you look at something, light from it enters your eye. It is focused by the lens. The light makes a picture or image on the part of your eye called the retina. Light enters a camera too. It is focused by a lens onto film. When light strikes the film in the camera it makes a record of what the camera sees.

■ **The eye and the camera**

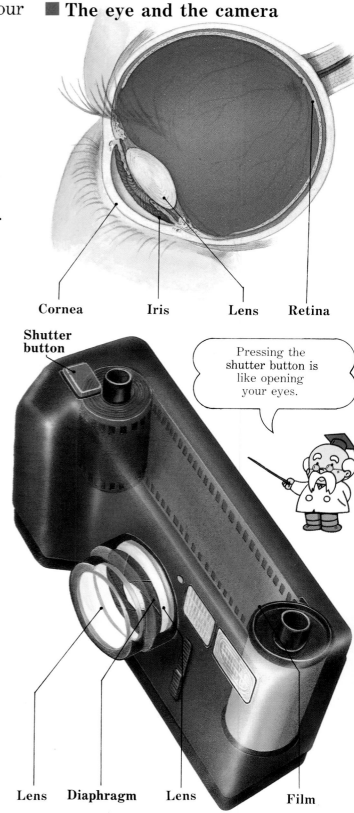

Cornea   Iris   Lens   Retina

Pressing the shutter button is like opening your eyes.

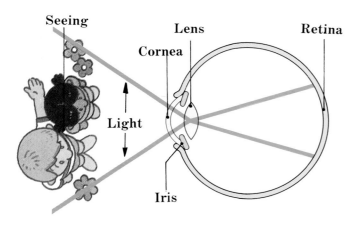

Seeing   Lens   Retina
Cornea
Light
Iris

The iris adjusts the amount of light that enters the eye. The lens focuses the image on the retina.

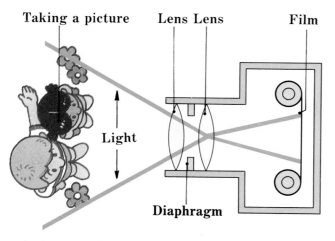

Taking a picture   Lens Lens   Film
Light
Diaphragm

An image on film is like the image on the retina, and the camera diaphragm works the way the iris does.

Shutter button

Lens   Diaphragm   Lens   Film

Then How Are Photographs Made From Film?

First the film has to be developed to make the image appear on the film. Next the image is printed on specially made paper that can be turned into a finished photo.

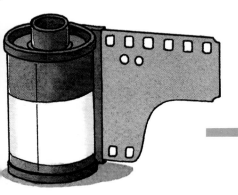

After you take a picture you can't see the image on the film.

The film is developed by using chemicals to make the image appear.

The colors of the object and the colors on the film are different.

Light passes through the film and puts the image on special paper.

When the paper is developed in chemicals the image appears.

Now the developed photo has the same colors as the real object

MINI-DATA

If you open your camera and light hits the film, the pictures on the film hit by the light will disappear.

• **To the Parent**

The basic system for a camera and for the human eye is the same, but the processing of images is quite different. The image projected on the retina of the eye is passed to the brain through the optic nerve. In the case of the camera, however, the image is recorded on film. Color negative film is covered with color couplers that record the colors of objects that are being photographed. The illustration on this page shows manual development, but processing usually is done by an autoprinter.

How Does a Copy Machine Work?

ANSWER A copy machine uses static electricity to make a copy of a piece of paper you place inside it. Static electricity is made up of positive and negative charges. In a copy machine the positive electric charges work like a magnet. They attract black powder called toner. The powder fills in all the spots to make a copy of the words and pictures on your paper.

▲ Copy machines can make large or small copies.

How a Copy Machine Makes Copies

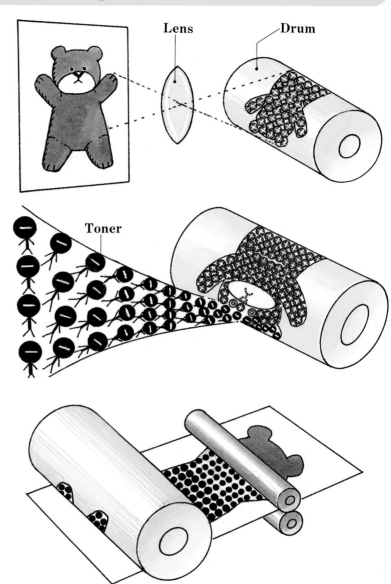

Lens   Drum

An image is made on the drum

When the copy machine's button is pushed a strong light hits the page that is to be copied. This light is reflected and then passes through the lens. This creates an image of the page on the outside of a turning cylinder drum. Because the image on this drum is created by positive charges of static electricity you cannot see it. Only the dark parts of the pictures and words on the page are positively charged.

Black powder does the job

Toner

Negatively charged black powder called toner is sprinkled on the image that has been projected on the copy machine's turning drum. The toner is attracted to the positive charges so a black picture is created on the drum. The toner is not attracted to the part that is not charged. This means that portion will remain white.

The picture goes onto paper

The picture made by the toner on the surface of the drum is transferred to the paper as the drum turns. The toner is a powder. By itself the toner cannot stick to the paper. So that the image will be printed, the paper passes between heated rollers. Like an iron, the heated rollers press and stick the toner in place and create the picture on the paper.

TRY THIS

It's easy to see how things that are positively and negatively charged will attract each other. One way to check this is to rub a plastic plate against your hair, then hold it close to a piece of paper. The paper will be attracted to the plastic. The reason is that the plastic plate is negatively charged and the paper is positively charged.

● To the Parent

The electronic copy machine uses static electricity when it makes copies. An object charged with static electricity is said to be electrified. In a copy machine the surface of the drum is coated with a substance called selenium, which can be electrified. High voltage is applied to the surface to give it a uniform positive charge. When the image to be copied is projected onto the surface of the drum the positive charge is removed from areas where the light strikes but is left on the drum's other areas.

How Can Sound Be Recorded on Tape?

ANSWER A tape recorder changes sound into electrical signals. Then it records those signals on a special kind of tape that can be made to act like a magnet.

Inside the tape recorder

Head

Recording tape

Battery

Cassette tape

The recording system

Recording tape is made of plastic with a thin coating of iron powder. The secret to recording sound on tape is in the iron powder. It can be magnetized, or changed into little magnets. The tape recorder changes sounds into electrical signals, and those magnetize the metal on the tape. That leaves magnetic signals on the tape, and these later can be changed back into sounds.

● To the Parent

The tape recorder records sound on a tape coated with powder containing a magnetic substance. Sound is changed into varying electric currents by a microphone. The current goes to the recording head and is changed into a varying magnetic force, which is recorded on the tape. Reversing the process, magnetic variations on the tape yield an electric current that speakers then convert into sound.

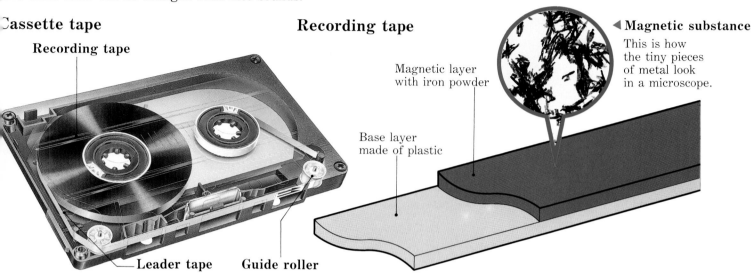

Cassette tape

Recording tape

Leader tape   Guide roller

Recording tape

Magnetic layer with iron powder

Base layer made of plastic

◀ **Magnetic substance**
This is how the tiny pieces of metal look in a microscope.

Sound is changed to electrical signals

During recording, the tape passes over a part called the head, which is really an electric magnet. The strength of the magnet changes depending on the strength of the electrical signals it receives from the microphone. As the tape passes over the head the iron powder in it is turned into magnets with the same magnetic strength as the head at that instant. Sound is recorded this way as changes in the strength of the tiny magnets on tape.

Recording head

Gap

Coil

Core

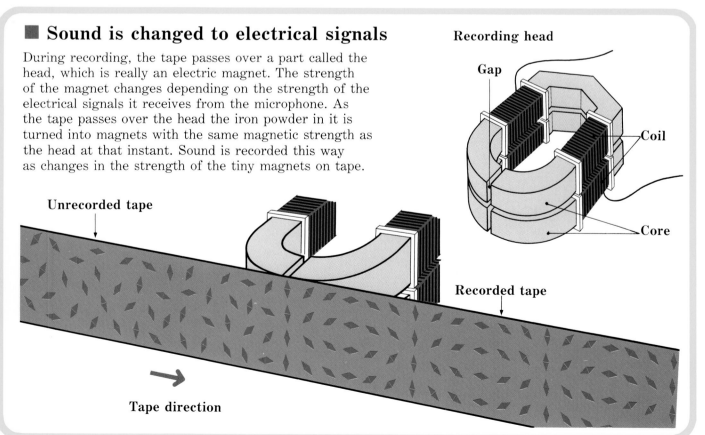

Unrecorded tape

Recorded tape

Tape direction

Changes in magnetic strength are shown as changes in the way the magnets line up.

❓ How Does a Radio Work?

ANSWER A radio station changes sound into electrical waves. It sends them out into the air. Our radio picks up those electrical waves and changes them back into sounds that we can hear.

■ **Radio station**

Mike
The microphone changes sound to electrical signals.

■ **Recording studio**
Recordings are put on tape in a studio like this.

The antenna on a radio picks up electrical waves from many stations. You tune in the station you want.

The electrical signals are removed from the wave you tune in.

■ Transmission antenna

The taller the antenna is, the farther it sends electrical waves.

Electrical waves from different stations

■ Transmission station

The station sends out electrical waves carrying radio signals into the air.

The speaker changes the signals into sounds.

Although we can't see them, electrical waves are sent out in various directions by a radio station. Radio waves travel at the speed of light, which is so fast it is hard to imagine. They go around the world seven times in a single second.

● **To the Parent**

Radio stations broadcast on various frequencies of electromagnetic waves. These include medium wave for standard AM broadcasts, short wave for overseas broadcasts, and very high frequency for stereo broadcasts on FM. The first commercial radio broadcast in the U.S. was made by station KDKA in Pittsburgh in 1920. At about the same time, government broadcast stations began operation in Europe. Radio broadcasting began in the Soviet Union in 1922, in Japan in 1925 and in India in 1926.

How Does a Music Box Make Music?

(ANSWER) Inside the box is a metal cylinder. It is covered with tiny bumps called pins. There is also a metal plate called a comb. When a spring turns the cylinder, the pins strike the teeth of the comb. That makes them vibrate and you hear music.

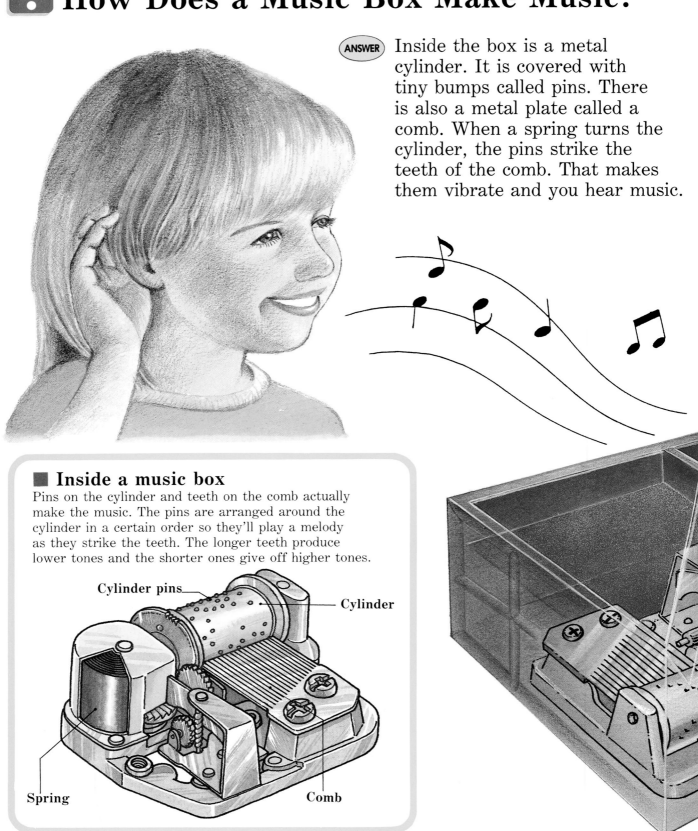

■ Inside a music box

Pins on the cylinder and teeth on the comb actually make the music. The pins are arranged around the cylinder in a certain order so they'll play a melody as they strike the teeth. The longer teeth produce lower tones and the shorter ones give off higher tones.

Cylinder pins

Cylinder

Spring

Comb

How the music is produced

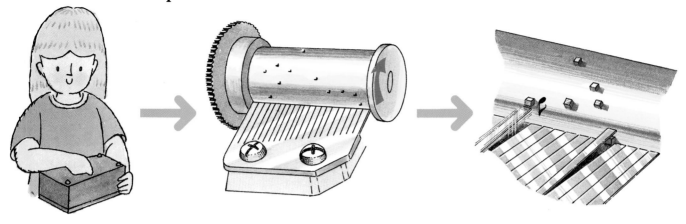

You may need to wind the spring first. If you do, be sure not to wind it up too tightly. Then open the cover of the music box.

In some music boxes the spring starts turning the cylinder when you open the cover. In others you have to flip a switch or lever.

As the cylinder turns, the pins strike some of the teeth in a certain order, making them vibrate so that they give off tones.

By themselves the pins and teeth produce a soft sound. The space in the wooden box makes these sounds louder, or amplifies them.

■ Electronic melody cards

Melody cards produce music when they're opened. When light strikes the tiny music box in the card, it starts playing music.

● To the Parent

A cylindrical drum in the music box is made to rotate by a spring-driven motor. There are pins on the drum positioned to strike the tuned teeth on the comb in a certain sequence, causing them to vibrate and produce a melody. In inexpensive music boxes the comb usually has 12 to 18 tuned teeth and plays only a brief piece of music that cannot be varied. But more expensive and elaborate music boxes may have between 50 and 140 teeth, with interchangeable cylinders to play rather long passages of music. If the mechanism is inside a wooden box or is placed on a wooden surface that serves as a sounding board, its sounds are amplified.

What Makes the Toast Pop Up In a Toaster?

ANSWER The secret to the toaster is a special switch located inside. It is made of two metals. As the toaster gets hot the heat on the two metals makes the switch begin to bend. When the toast is ready the bending switch shuts off the electricity. At the same time the switch triggers a spring that makes the toast pop up.

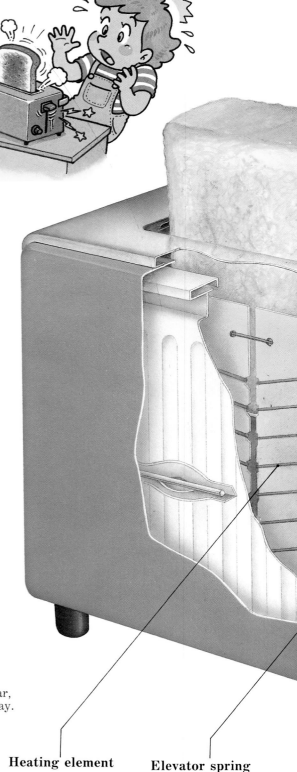

■ How it works

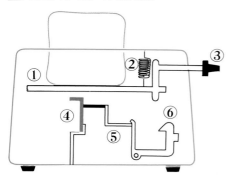

① Bread rack
② Spring
③ Switch lever
④ Metal switch
⑤ Push bar
⑥ Hook

Bread is held in the rack.

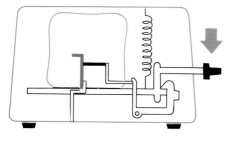

When you push the lever down it lowers the bread and turns the heater on. The heat toasts the bread.

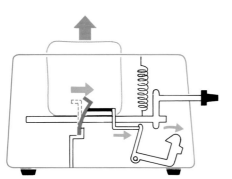

The heat also makes the metal switch bend. The switch touches the push bar, which pushes the hook away. That releases the spring, which pushes the toast up.

Heating element   Elevator spring

The secret of a toaster switch

Metal expands when it is heated, but each kind of metal expands a different amount. A bimetal switch is made of two kinds of metal. One of them will expand more than the other, so the switch bends when it heats up.

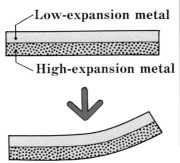

Low-expansion metal

High-expansion metal

It bends toward the low-expansion metal.

▲ The top bar is cold.

▲ When it's heated it bends.

Other appliances that use bimetal switches

Refrigerators, irons and other home appliances use bimetal switches to keep their temperature constant.

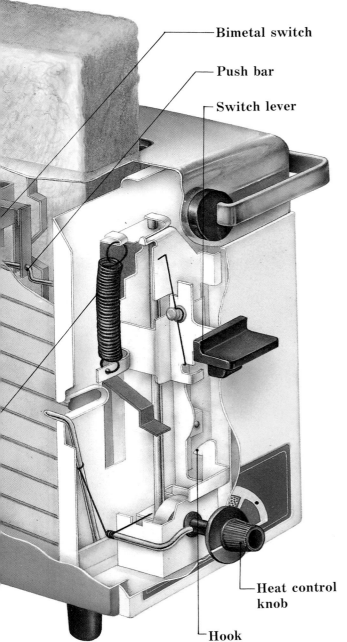

Bimetal switch

Push bar

Switch lever

Heat control knob

Hook

Iron

Foot warmer

Refrigerator

● **To the Parent**

In a bimetal device two pieces of metal with different rates of thermal expansion are laminated together to form one plate. When heated the plate bends toward the side with the lower expansion rate. When cooled it reverts to its original shape. Most bimetal devices use brass for high expansion and an alloy called invar for low expansion. A very common device of this type is the thermostat, which switches current on and off to maintain a set temperature.

How Does a Microwave Oven Cook Food?

(ANSWER) The oven has a machine called a magnetron. It sends out microwaves, which make the tiny water particles in food move around. When these particles rub against each other it makes heat. That cooks the food.

Waveguide
Microwaves are guided into the heating chamber

Magnetron
Microwaves are produced here.

Heating chamb

Microwaves

Turntable
Food is turned so that it will heat uniformly.

Timer switch

■ The food isn't browned

Microwaves cook by heating up the water on the surface or inside the food. With microwaves alone the food doesn't turn brown, just as it doesn't brown when it is steamed. Some microwave ovens have another kind of heater that will brown the food after it's cooked by the microwaves. That way the food looks more appetizing.

Food will burn when heat is applied to it directly. With microwaves the food isn't browned even though it's cooked.

Some Facts About Microwaves

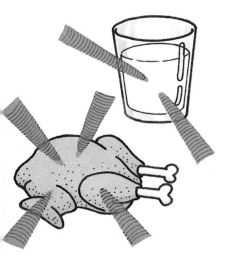

Microwaves are drawn to foods that contain water.

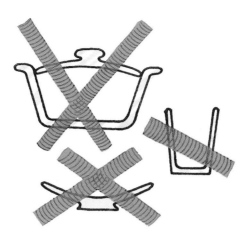

Microwaves can pass right through materials like glass or china.

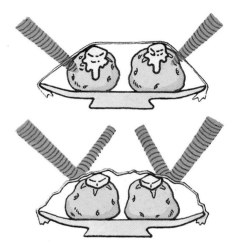

They go through plastic wrap but are reflected by aluminum foil.

Why Do Microwaves Make Water Particles Hot?

Water particles, or molecules, vibrate and move around when they are hit by microwaves. These particles have uneven shapes, so when they rub against other molecules they produce friction and a great deal of heat.

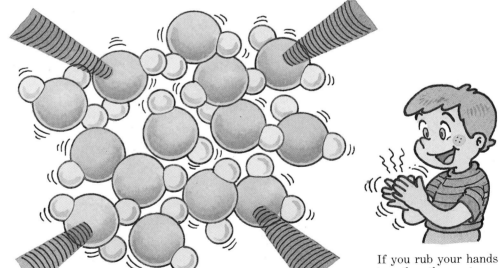

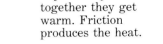

If you rub your hands together they get warm. Friction produces the heat.

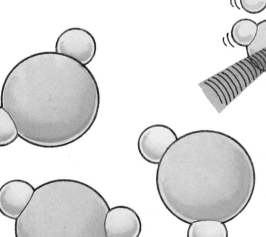

Water molecules have uneven shapes.

● To the Parent

The electric wave that is produced by the magnetron in a microwave oven oscillates at an extremely high frequency. The actual vibration rate is about 2.45 billion times per second. This kind of electric wave is what is known as a microwave. When a water molecule is exposed to a microwave it becomes excited and vibrates the same number of times per second that the microwave does. Vibration of molecules generates a tremendous amount of heat, and that cooks food.

How Does a Vacuum Cleaner Pick Up Dust?

ANSWER Put a straw in a glass of juice and take a drink. As you suck the air out, the straw fills with juice. A vacuum cleaner works this way too. As the vacuum sucks out the air it pulls in dirt and dust.

● **Suction head**
Place the suction head right over the dust, waste or anything else you want to clean up. You can use heads of different sizes depending on where you want to clean.

● **Collector**
This is where the dirt and dust collect. Some vacuum cleaners use a paper bag here that can be thrown away when it gets full.

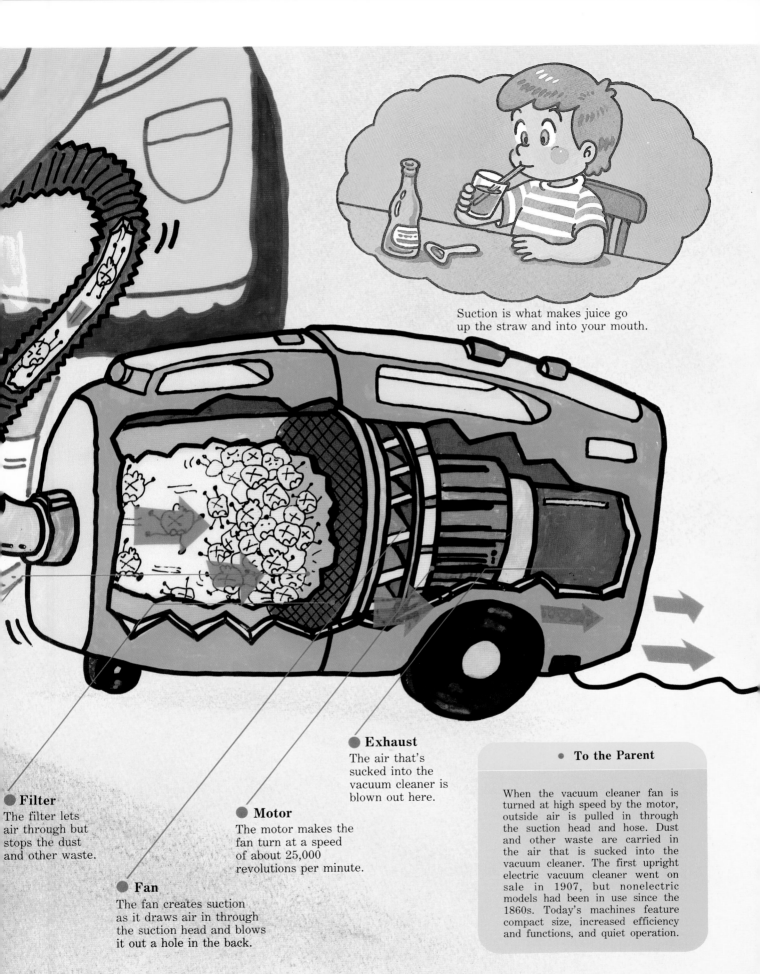

Suction is what makes juice go up the straw and into your mouth.

Exhaust
The air that's sucked into the vacuum cleaner is blown out here.

Filter
The filter lets air through but stops the dust and other waste.

Fan
The fan creates suction as it draws air in through the suction head and blows it out a hole in the back.

Motor
The motor makes the fan turn at a speed of about 25,000 revolutions per minute.

To the Parent

When the vacuum cleaner fan is turned at high speed by the motor, outside air is pulled in through the suction head and hose. Dust and other waste are carried in the air that is sucked into the vacuum cleaner. The first upright electric vacuum cleaner went on sale in 1907, but nonelectric models had been in use since the 1860s. Today's machines feature compact size, increased efficiency and functions, and quiet operation.

39

How Do Thermometers Tell Us What the Temperature Is?

(ANSWER) Inside a thermometer is a liquid. It may be mercury or alcohol. As the weather gets warmer this liquid takes up more space. The only place it can go is up the glass tube. As the level goes up it we are able to read the changing temperature. When it cools, the liquid takes up less space and drops down. We read this change as a drop in the temperature.

Alcohol expands as the temperature rises.

It contracts as the temperature drops.

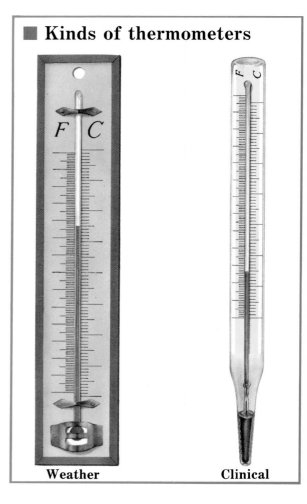

Kinds of thermometers

Weather

Clinical

Why Do You Have to Shake a Clinical Thermometer To Make the Mercury Fall?

In a clinical thermometer, which measures body temperature, the mercury doesn't fall after it rises. It's held in place by a narrow point in the thermometer. You have to shake the thermometer to make the mercury fall below that narrow point. If the mercury rose and fell with the air temperature, it would start falling as soon as it was removed from your body. And if it did that, it wouldn't really be showing what your body temperature was.

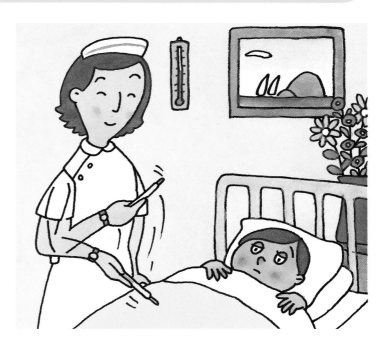

The narrow part is here.

A map of body temperatures

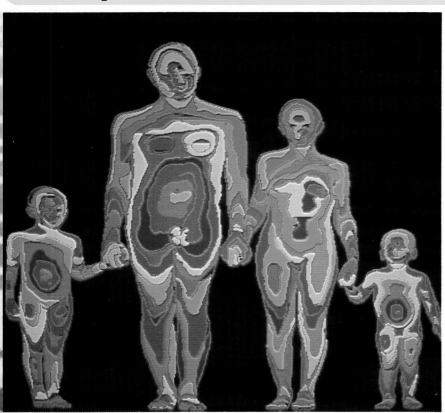

▲ Here colors show the differences in body temperatures.

The temperature of the human body isn't the same for all parts of the body. A thermograph is a kind of computer that uses different colors to show differences in temperature for each body part. Red shows the parts with high temperature and blue indicates the parts with low temperature.

● To the Parent

Thermometers work on the principle that the volume of a substance increases or decreases according to changes in its temperature. Metals, gases and liquids are used to make thermometers. Mercury and dyed alcohol are most commonly used for filling thermometers. Most countries use the Celsius scale under which 0° and 100° respectively represent freezing and boiling temperatures of water. In the U.S. the Fahrenheit scale (32° freezing, 212° boiling) is still the most commonly used.

❓ Why Does an X-ray Photograph Show Only Bones?

ANSWER When you are X-rayed, invisible waves pass through you. They go through your skin, muscles and organs, but can't go through your bones. That's why your bones can be seen on an X-ray photograph.

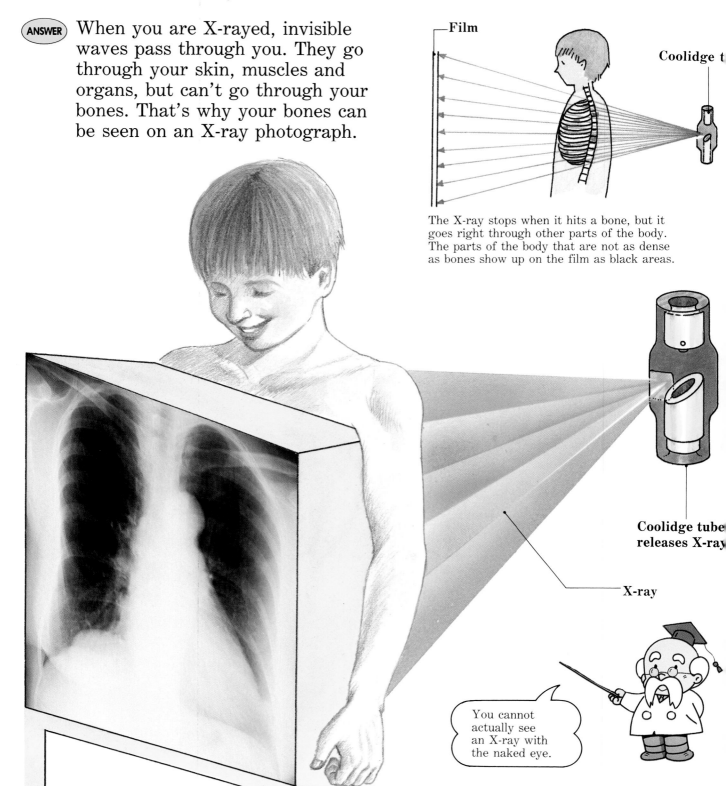

Film

Coolidge t

The X-ray stops when it hits a bone, but it goes right through other parts of the body. The parts of the body that are not as dense as bones show up on the film as black areas.

Coolidge tube
releases X-ray

X-ray

You cannot actually see an X-ray with the naked eye.

This picture shows an X-ray image as if it had already been developed. Actually the film must be developed to see the image.

So How Do They Take X-ray Pictures Of a Person's Stomach?

When a person's stomach is to be X-rayed, the person must drink a special liquid that stops X-rays. The photo is taken while the inside of the stomach is coated with liquid.

The liquid tastes bad, but it helps guard your health.

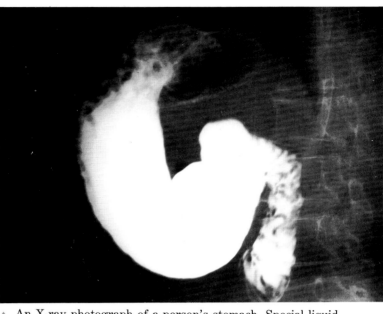

▲ An X-ray photograph of a person's stomach. Special liquid helps to make a clear picture of the stomach's shape.

Are there other ways to use X-ray photographs?

An X-ray image can be taken of an ancient sword or other old objects so that any letters or markings that have been worn away can be seen.

When a picture has been painted over another picture, an X-ray photograph can be made that lets us see the picture underneath.

An X-ray photograph can be made of an object such as a statue to make it possible to see what is inside it without damaging the figure.

● To the Parent

X-rays are electromagnetic waves that go through elements with low atomic numbers. They will not pass through bones, which are primarily phosphorous and calcium, with atomic numbers 15 and 20. They will pass through internal organs, which are mostly hydrogen, carbon and oxygen, with atomic numbers of 1, 6 and 8.

? How Does a Flashlight Work?

ANSWER A flashlight has batteries and a light bulb. When the switch is turned on, electricity that's stored in the batteries flows through the bulb and makes it light up.

■ Parts of a flashlight

Light bulb

Reflector
Focuses the light toward the front

18

Switch

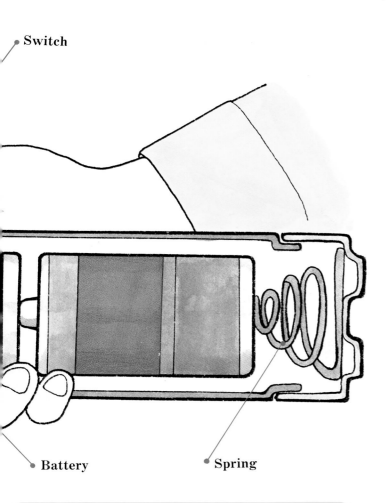

Battery   **Spring**

■ Batteries come in different sizes

Flashlight batteries come in several sizes, but all of them are 1½ volts. The larger the battery's size, the longer it can supply enough electricity to run a flashlight, a portable radio or a cassette player.

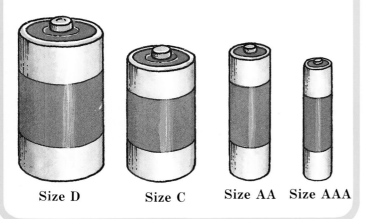

Size D   Size C   Size AA Size AAA

■ Kinds of flashlights

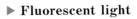

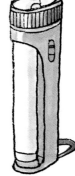

◄ **Cap light**
Wearing this flashlight on your head leaves both your hands free.

► **Fluorescent light**
With this flashlight you can use either a fluorescent light or a regular light bulb.

◄ **Radio light**
Listen to the news.

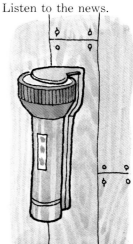

► **Emergency light**
Remove this flashlight from the holder and it turns itself on.

▲ **Penlight**
It fits in your pocket.

● To the Parent

Because the flashlight is a simple mechanism and uses current at a safe, low level, it is a good device to illustrate the basic operation of other electrical equipment. Help the child remove the batteries, turn them around and replace them in the flashlight to see if it still works. Point out the circuits connecting to plus and minus battery poles.

How Does a Battery Make Electricity?

ANSWER Look carefully at a dry cell battery. You may see a plus sign located near the top of it and a minus sign near the bottom. These mark the battery's two poles. Inside the battery is a special mixture of chemicals. These release tiny particles called electrons. When you connect the poles of the battery with wire, the electrons flow from one pole to the other. We call this flow electricity.

■ Dry-cell battery

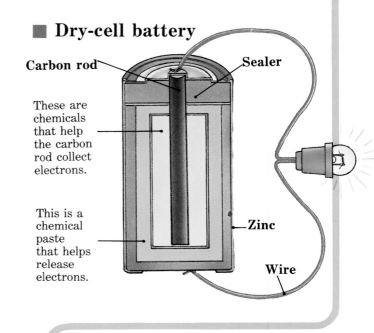

Carbon rod

Sealer

These are chemicals that help the carbon rod collect electrons.

This is a chemical paste that helps release electrons.

Zinc

Wire

MINI-DATA

You may be surprised at some of the things around you that can be used to produce electricity. A lemon is a good example. When a zinc and a copper strip are put in a lemon, the lemon juice causes the zinc to release electrons. If the zinc and copper are connected by wire, electrons will begin to flow in an electrical current. A lemon can produce only a very tiny amount of electricity. We can measure it by using an instrument called an ammeter. Electricians use this same instrument to test the flow of an electric current when they repair a circuit.

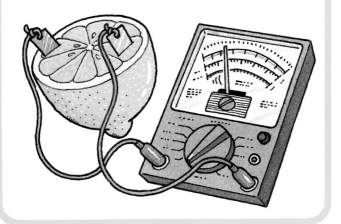

■ How a battery works

1 Chemicals turn zinc atoms into zinc ions. Each atom releases two electrons.

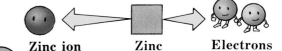

Zinc ion   Zinc   Electrons

2 The electrons travel through the wire toward the carbon rod.

3 Each electron unites with a hydrogen ion to form a bubble of hydrogen gas.

Electron   Hydrogen ion   Hydrogen gas

4 Hydrogen gas joins with oxygen to form water.

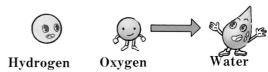

Hydrogen   Oxygen   Water

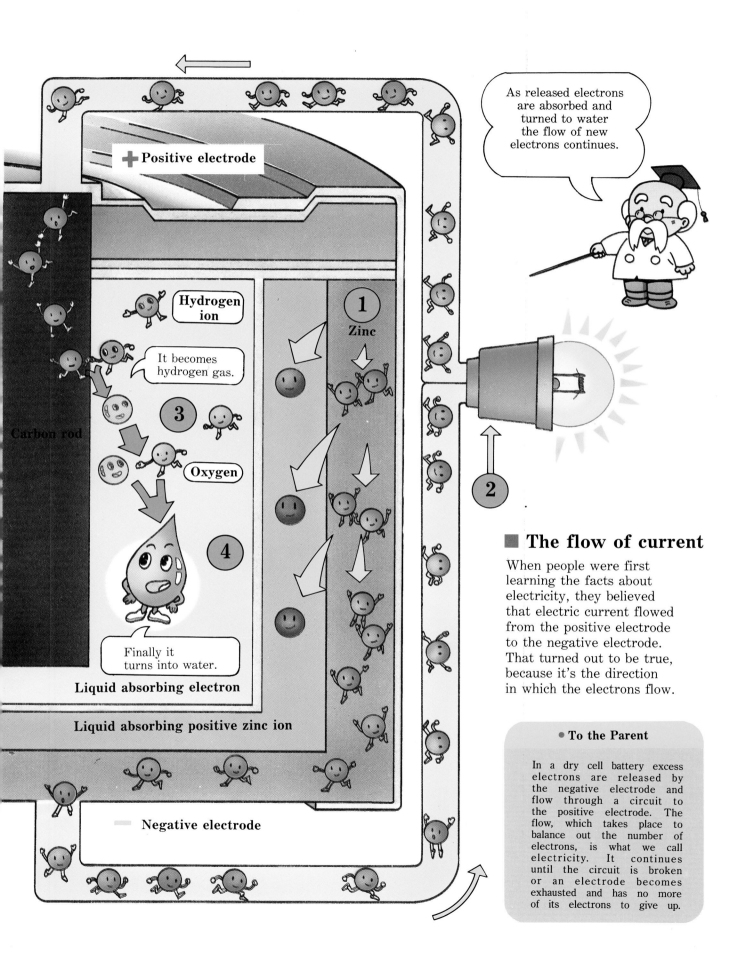

As released electrons are absorbed and turned to water the flow of new electrons continues.

+ **Positive electrode**

Hydrogen ion

It becomes hydrogen gas.

1

Zinc

3

Oxygen

4

Finally it turns into water.

Carbon rod

Liquid absorbing electron

Liquid absorbing positive zinc ion

2

— **Negative electrode**

■ The flow of current

When people were first learning the facts about electricity, they believed that electric current flowed from the positive electrode to the negative electrode. That turned out to be true, because it's the direction in which the electrons flow.

● **To the Parent**

In a dry cell battery excess electrons are released by the negative electrode and flow through a circuit to the positive electrode. The flow, which takes place to balance out the number of electrons, is what we call electricity. It continues until the circuit is broken or an electrode becomes exhausted and has no more of its electrons to give up.

![?] How Does a Bicycle Headlight Work?

ANSWER Some bicycle lights are connected by wire to a generator. This source of power touches one of the wheels. When the wheel turns, the generator can produce enough electricity to make the bicycle light work.

■ Inside the generator

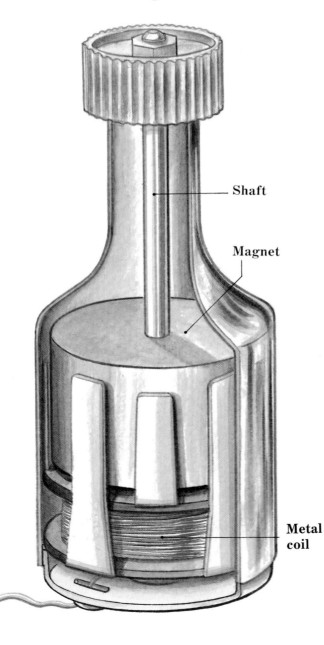

Shaft

Magnet

Metal coil

▲ Bicycle generator and headlight

48

How Is the Electricity Produced?

When the generator is released and touches the tire, the tire makes the generator shaft turn.

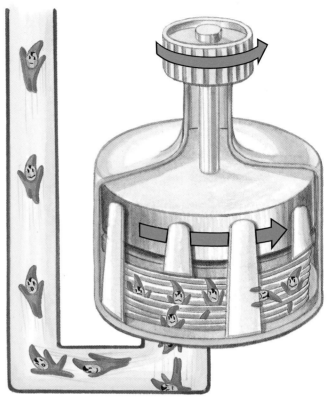

The shaft has a magnet at one end. When the magnet turns inside the coil a flow of electricity is produced.

TRY THIS

If you pedal slowly, the tire turns slowly and so does the generator shaft. Only a little electricity is generated, so the headlight is very dim. But as you pedal faster and generate more electricity, the headlight gets brighter and brighter.

Try this with a friend, but do it in a safe place where there isn't any traffic.

● **To the Parent**

A bicycle's generator produces electricity by the rotation of the bicycle's tire. A permanent magnet attached to the generator shaft is rotated by a wheel that comes in contact with the tire, and the magnetic field around the rotating magnet induces alternating electric current in the generator coil. There usually is only one wire connecting the generator and the headlight because both are grounded to the bicycle frame, which provides a return path for the electricity.

? Why Does the Face of a Clock Glow in the Dark?

ANSWER The hands and numbers are covered with special paint, which gives off a small amount of light all the time. You can't see it in daylight because the regular light is so bright. But at night you can see it glowing.

MINI-DATA

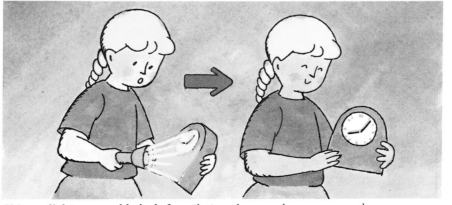

Shine a light on an old clock face that no longer glows very much. Even though it's old, the paint will glow brightly for a while.

Luminous paint glows because it has special chemicals in it. The chemicals can store up light and release it, too. That's what causes the glow you see. But when the paint gets old those chemicals become weak, and they don't work as well.

■ Why luminous paint glows

In the sunlight zinc sulfide stores light

Zinc sulfide glows as it releases stored light.

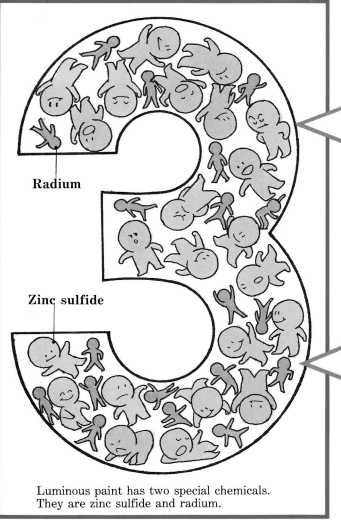

Radium

Zinc sulfide

Luminous paint has two special chemicals. They are zinc sulfide and radium.

The radium is what makes the zinc sulfide release the light that it has stored.

■ Luminous paint is often used on watches too

▲ In daylight you can't see the glow of a watch that has a luminous dial.

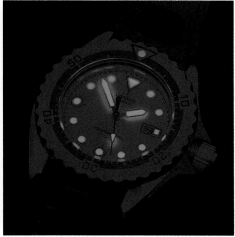

▲ But in the dark you will be able to see the watch glowing dimly.

● To the Parent

Luminous paint contains powdered zinc sulfide and grains of radium, with about one part radium per thousand parts of zinc sulfide. The zinc sulfide has the ability to store some of the light to which it is exposed. Normally all the accumulated light would be released in about 20 minutes. However, the radium in the paint gives off radiation that controls the rate at which light is released by the zinc sulfide. Luminous paint usually glows for about three to eight years, with the strength of the glow decreasing as the radium becomes weaker and weaker.

Why Do Fluorescent Bulbs Flicker?

(ANSWER) When we flip their switch, an electric discharge shoots through a glass tube. In a fluorescent light there is a space without wire. It takes a moment for the electricity to build up and flow here, so the light flickers.

■ Fluorescent light system

You can see a coiled wire at each end of the fluorescent light bulb. When the switch is turned on a flow of invisible electrons shoots from one wire pole to the other one. The electrons are passing through a part of the bulb which is filled with mercury gas. This produces the radiation that we see as light.

A starter and a stabilizer are needed to make a fluorescent light work. These produce the flow of electrons and make sure it continues.

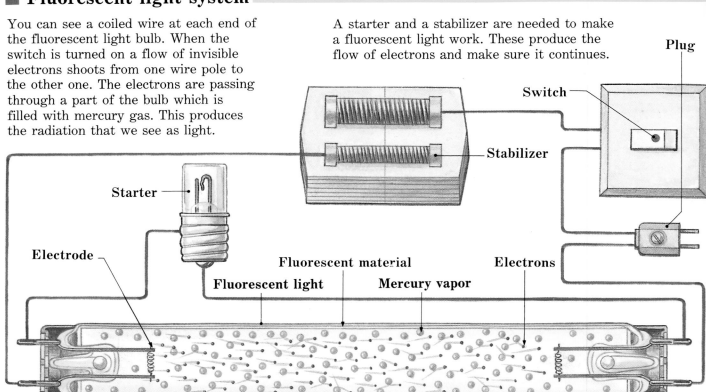

Plug

Switch

Stabilizer

Starter

Electrode

Fluorescent material

Fluorescent light

Mercury vapor

Electrons

How a starter lights a bulb

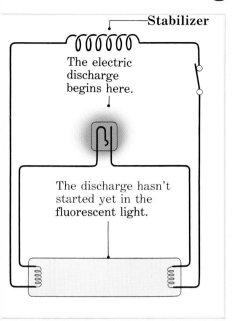

Stabilizer

The electric discharge begins here.

The discharge hasn't started yet in the fluorescent light.

When the switch is turned on, the discharge begins in the starter. The heat from the discharge makes the wires there bend toward each other.

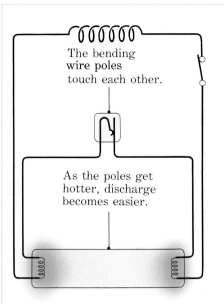

The bending wire poles touch each other.

As the poles get hotter, discharge becomes easier.

When the electric poles in the starter touch each other the discharge stops, but the electric current then flows to the lamp's electric poles, which get hot.

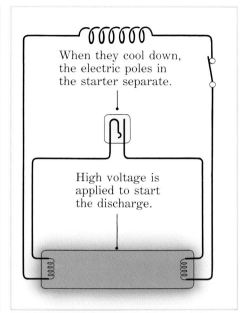

When they cool down, the electric poles in the starter separate.

High voltage is applied to start the discharge.

When the starter cools down after discharge ends, its electric poles separate. This sends high voltage to the fluorescent lamp's electric poles, and its discharge begins.

Why Do Fluorescent Bulbs Produce White Light?

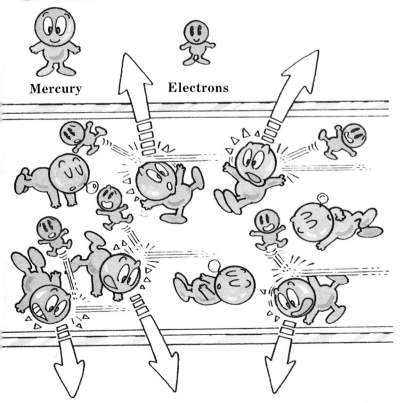

Mercury   Electrons

The inside of the fluorescent light contains mercury. When discharge starts and heat is generated the mercury changes into a gas, which fills the tube. Electrons shooting between the electric poles hit the mercury gas, producing ultraviolet radiation. The human eye can't see this kind of radiation, but when it touches the fluorescent material with which the inside of the fluorescent light is coated, it changes to white light. That's why fluorescent bulbs produce white light.

● **To the Parent**

A fluorescent light does not produce light immediately because it takes time to apply high voltage to its electric poles and so start the discharge between them. The starter and the stabilizer generate this voltage. When discharge in the starter ends, the two bimetallic electric poles inside it shrink and separate. The circuit opens, generating voltage in the stabilizer's coil that goes to the fluorescent light's electric poles.

? How Is a Neon Sign's Color Produced?

ANSWER A neon light works the same basic way as a fluorescent light with one very important difference. Instead of being filled with mercury gas, these tubes have either neon or argon gas. When electric current flows through these gases they produce red light and blue light. By combining these with tubes made of colored glass we produce beautiful signs.

When neon is bright

The neon in a neon tube can't be seen with the naked eye because it is in very small particles called atoms. When an atom is hit by an even smaller particle called an electron, the atom discharges some light.

Neon atom   **Electrons**

Some colorful neon tubes

A green neon tube

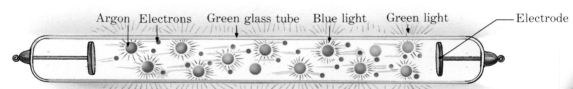

Argon   Electrons   Green glass tube   Blue light   Green light — Electrode

If electrons hit argon it emits blue light, which turns green if put through a green glass tube.

A red neon tube

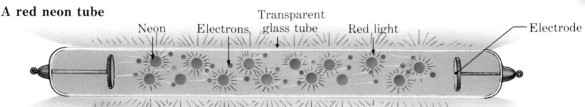

Neon   Electrons   Transparent glass tube   Red light — Electrode

When electrons hit neon it emits red light. Since the tube is transparent the light stays red.

A blue neon tube

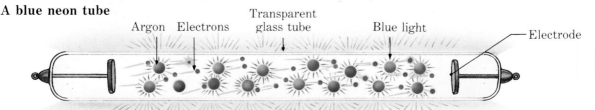

Argon   Electrons   Transparent glass tube   Blue light — Electrode

When electrons hit argon it releases blue light. Green, red and blue are the most popular neon colors.

54

▲ **Neon sign.** The tubes have been shaped into a design.

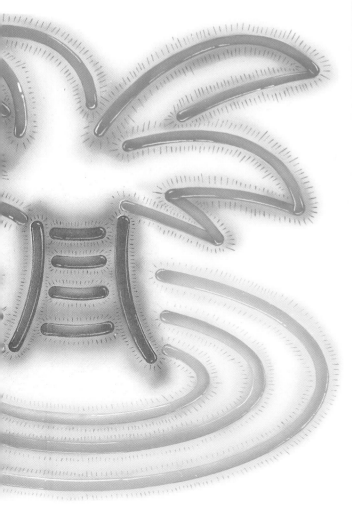

▲ **Neon cowboy.** Its neon tubes release various colors.

● **To the Parent**

When an electron comes into contact with a neon atom, the atom gives off bright light for a moment. This is because electrons moving around the nucleus of the neon atom are displaced by electrons produced by the neon tube's electrode. When these displaced electrons are restored to their original trajectory, the energy that is left over is discharged in the form of light.

❓ How Does an Escalator Work?

ANSWER Just stand on an escalator step, and it will carry you upward or downward. As each step reaches the end of its run it folds inward and moves back to the escalator's starting point.

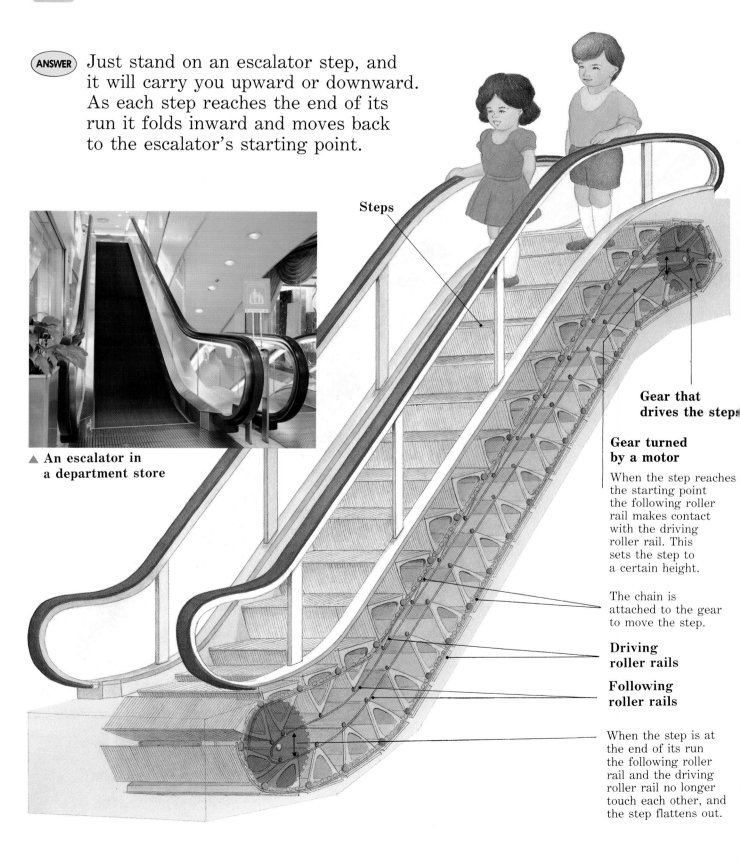

▲ An escalator in a department store

Steps

Gear that drives the step

Gear turned by a motor

When the step reaches the starting point the following roller rail makes contact with the driving roller rail. This sets the step to a certain height.

The chain is attached to the gear to move the step.

Driving roller rails

Following roller rails

When the step is at the end of its run the following roller rail and the driving roller rail no longer touch each other, and the step flattens out.

What Makes An Elevator Work?

An elevator has a place for people to ride, called a car, and a heavy weight to balance it. The car and weight are attached by a wire rope.

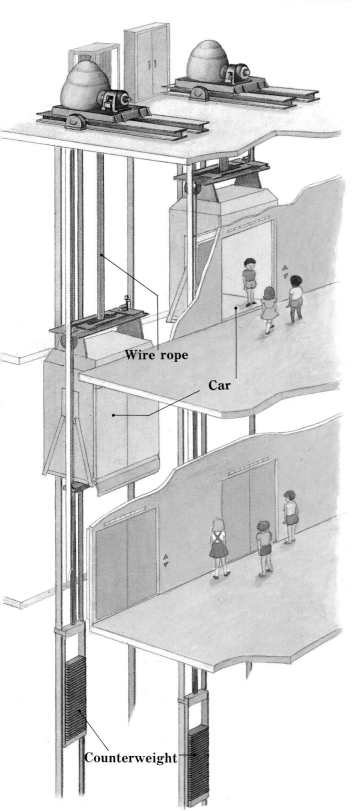

Wire rope

Car

Counterweight

▲ **Sears Tower.** This Chicago building is the tallest in the world. It has 110 floors and 103 elevators.

● **To the Parent**

An escalator travels at between 80 and 100 feet (24.4 and 30.5 m) per minute and can carry between 5,000 and 8,000 people per hour, depending on how wide its steps are. Its transport capacity per floor is several times an elevator's. Various safety measures are taken to make elevators safe. For example there is an emergency braking device that keeps the elevator from falling if the wire rope breaks.

Why Do We Face Backward When We Row?

ANSWER In a rowboat we use two oars. As we push the flat ends of these paddles back through the water the boat moves forward. We want to use as much of our energy as possible to push the water. By facing backward we use more of our muscle power and the boat moves easily.

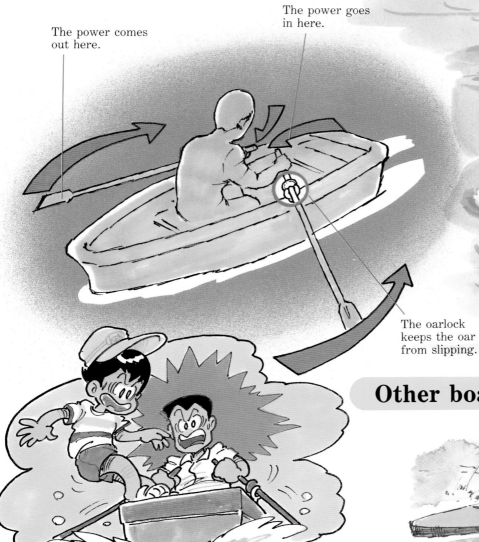

The power comes out here.

The power goes in here.

The oarlock keeps the oar from slipping.

Standing up in a boat is dangerous because the boat could turn over!

Other boats with oars

▲ **Kayak.** Paddles that are flat at both ends are used, and rowers face forward.

How to Row a Boat

When both hands produce the same amount of power, the boat moves straight ahead.

When only the oar in the right hand is used, the boat turns to its right.

When only the oar in the left hand is used, the boat turns to its left.

Canoe. Using a paddle that is flat at one end, rowers crouch on one knee and face forward.

● **To the Parent**

The leverage principle can be understood from how a boat is rowed. The oar is the lever. The point where the oar is attached to the boat is the fulcrum. The point where power goes in is the power point. The point where the oar hits the water is the application point. With a racing boat the end of the oar is the fulcrum and the point where the oar is attached to the boat is the point of application. Not all boats are rowed this way. Canoes and kayaks are rowed facing forward. Paddles for canoes are flat on one end, but those for kayaks are flat on both ends.

? How Does a Car Engine Work?

ANSWER A car's engine has many parts. When gasoline burns, energy moves a part called the piston up and down. This sends power to a system of connecting parts. When this force reaches the wheels it makes them turn. You can see how a piston works in the drawings below.

◀ **A car's engine**
This is a big engine. It has eight cylinders and pistons arranged in the form of the letter V, so it is called a V-8 engine.

■ **How a 4-cycle engine works**

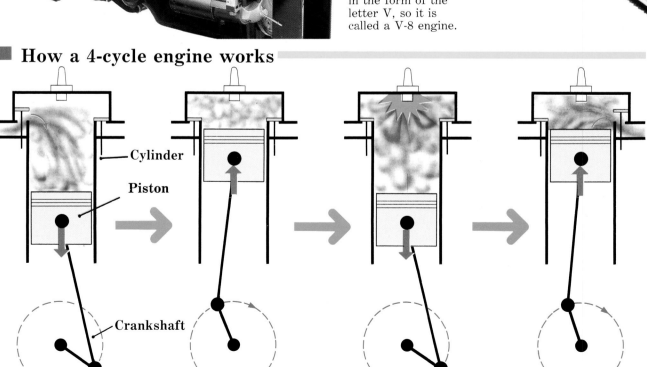

Cylinder

Piston

Crankshaft

The piston moves down and pulls a mixture of air and gasoline into the cylinder.

The piston moves up and compresses the air and gasoline mixture in the cylinder.

The compressed mixture fires. That forces the piston down and makes the crankshaft go around.

The piston moves back up, forcing waste from the burned gasoline out of the cylinder.

Wow! I want to go riding!

●To the Parent

An automobile engine is an internal-combustion engine, which burns fuel within its cylinders. The engine shown here is a reciprocating engine. In such an engine the energy transferred by pistons moving up and down is changed by the crankshaft into the rotary motion. In a four-cycle engine the crankshaft makes two revolutions, powered by movement of the pistons, to accomplish each cycle's four phases of injection, compression, combustion and exhaust. The Wankel engine is another type of internal-combustion engine. It does not depend on pistons moving up and down. Instead the exploding gasoline's energy is used to turn a rotor, and that rotation is transferred directly to the wheels.

The engine is such an important part of a car that it is called the heart of the car.

An engine

Why Does a Power Shovel Have So Much Strength?

ANSWER A power shovel uses a very powerful engine. This engine has a pump filled with oil that pushes and pulls to make the shovel scoop up dirt and load it on trucks.

How do the arm and bucket move?

Powerful cylinders make the arm and bucket turn and move. They work a little like the muscles in our arm and hand.

When Cylinder 1 moves, the boom goes up or down. When Cylinder 2 is operated, power is transferred to the arm. When Cylinder 3 is used, power is transferred to the bucket, and it digs up the ground.

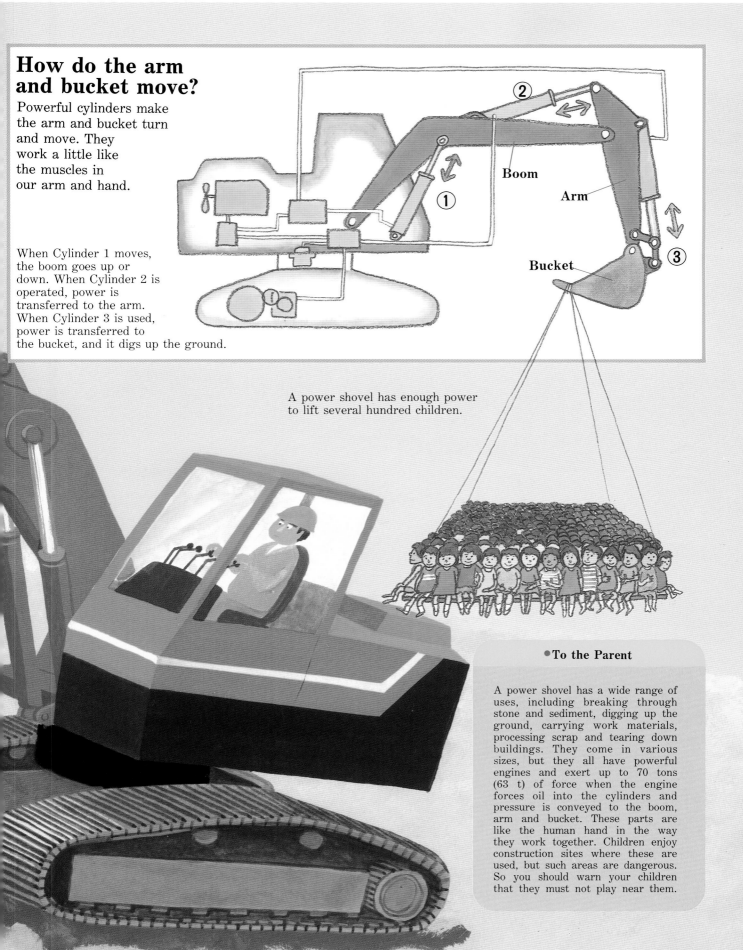

Boom

Arm

Bucket

A power shovel has enough power to lift several hundred children.

● To the Parent

A power shovel has a wide range of uses, including breaking through stone and sediment, digging up the ground, carrying work materials, processing scrap and tearing down buildings. They come in various sizes, but they all have powerful engines and exert up to 70 tons (63 t) of force when the engine forces oil into the cylinders and pressure is conveyed to the boom, arm and bucket. These parts are like the human hand in the way they work together. Children enjoy construction sites where these are used, but such areas are dangerous. So you should warn your children that they must not play near them.

How Can a Crane Lift Very Heavy Things?

ANSWER A crane has pulleys and gears to lift heavy things. It uses only a little power.

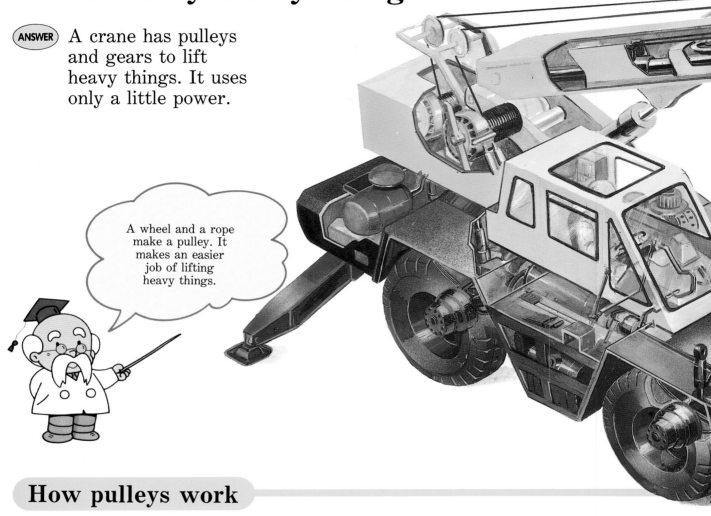

A wheel and a rope make a pulley. It makes an easier job of lifting heavy things.

How pulleys work

▼ It is not easy to lift this by hand.

◀ It can be lifted more easily if a pulley is used.

◀ If two pulleys are used it is very easy to lift the same load.

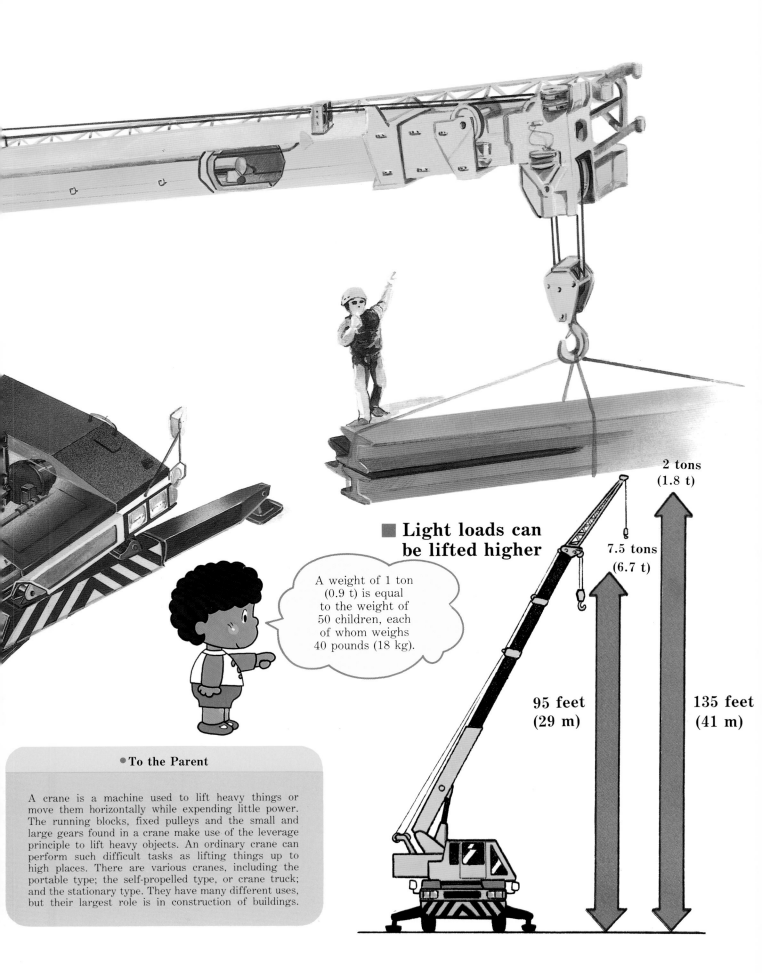

■ Light loads can be lifted higher

A weight of 1 ton (0.9 t) is equal to the weight of 50 children, each of whom weighs 40 pounds (18 kg).

2 tons (1.8 t)

7.5 tons (6.7 t)

95 feet (29 m)

135 feet (41 m)

● To the Parent

A crane is a machine used to lift heavy things or move them horizontally while expending little power. The running blocks, fixed pulleys and the small and large gears found in a crane make use of the leverage principle to lift heavy objects. An ordinary crane can perform such difficult tasks as lifting things up to high places. There are various cranes, including the portable type; the self-propelled type, or crane truck; and the stationary type. They have many different uses, but their largest role is in construction of buildings.

❓ How Do Brakes Stop a Train?

ANSWER You may be surprised to know that air makes a train's brakes work. This air is kept under pressure so it is called compressed air. When the engineer pulls the brake lever, air flows into and presses against the brake cylinders. This moves the brake shoe into place to slow down or stop the wheels from turning.

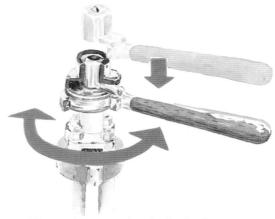

The engineer carries the brake lever with him. When he sits down in the driver's seat, he puts the lever in place. When he is finished driving he removes it and takes it with him.

■ Brake system

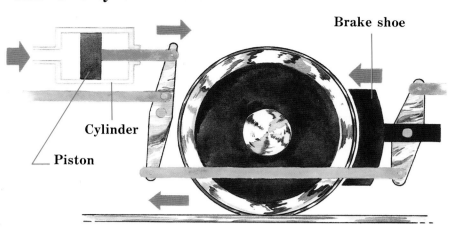

Brake shoe

Cylinder

Piston

When compressed air is transferred to the cylinder it pushes against the piston. The motion of the piston is transferred by levers, which press the brake shoe against the wheel to stop it.

■ Disk brake system

If this system's brake shoes are pressed directly against the wheels, the wheels will get hot and may be damaged. So a disk is attached to the axle, and the brake shoe presses against that instead of against the wheel.

Disk

Air is powerful

When air is forced into a narrow space, it pushes in all directions. Air brakes utilize this compressed power.

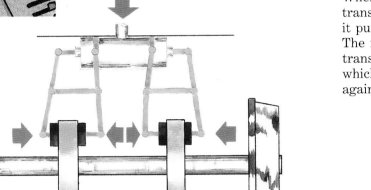

● **To the Parent**

Trains use air, electric and manual brakes. Air brakes send compressed air to the brake cylinder, where the air pushes against a piston. This power is amplified by a series of levers, which press the brake shoe against the wheel to brake it. If the brake shoe is pressed directly against the wheel it is a tread brake. If the brake shoe is pressed against a disk attached to the axle on which the wheel turns, rather than directly to the wheel itself, it is referred to as a disk brake.

What Happens to Old Cars?

ANSWER When a car becomes too old or too damaged to be used anymore it is crushed into a big steel cube. The machine that does this is called a scrap processor. The cube of steel is then melted and made into other steel products.

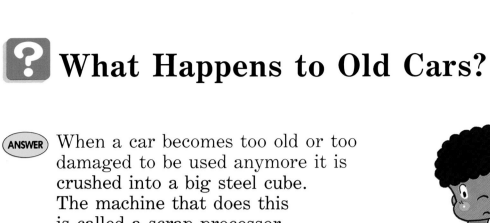

Lid

Pushing cylinder

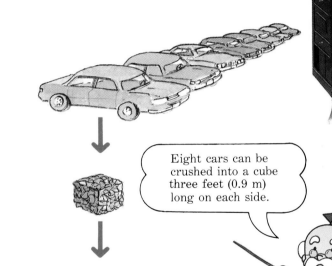

Eight cars can be crushed into a cube three feet (0.9 m) long on each side.

■ Crushing cars (seen from above)

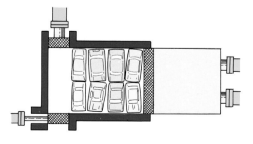

The old cars are put into the compression chamber.

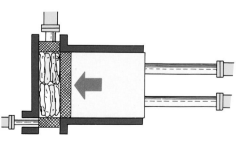

The cars are crushed by the main cylinder, which uses as much as 2,500 tons (2,250 t) of force.

The cylinder has a force of up to 1,800 tons (1,620 t).

Crushing: start to finish

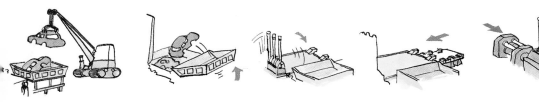

The first step:
a crane puts the
car into the box.

The car is
dumped into the
compression chamber.

Then the lid
is put on the
compression chamber.

The car is
crushed by the
main cylinder.

The pushing
cylinder crushes
from the sides.

The cube of
steel leaves
the chamber.

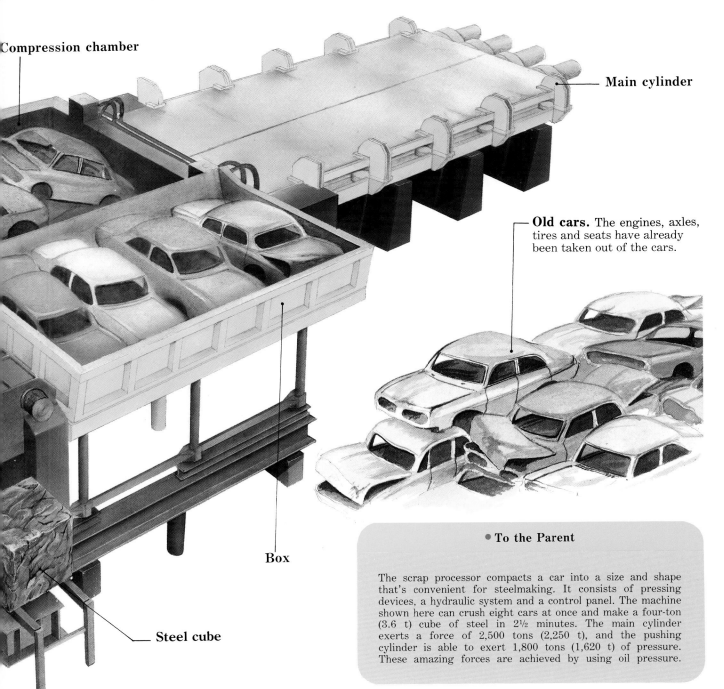

Compression chamber

Main cylinder

Old cars. The engines, axles,
tires and seats have already
been taken out of the cars.

Box

Steel cube

• To the Parent

The scrap processor compacts a car into a size and shape
that's convenient for steelmaking. It consists of pressing
devices, a hydraulic system and a control panel. The machine
shown here can crush eight cars at once and make a four-ton
(3.6 t) cube of steel in 2½ minutes. The main cylinder
exerts a force of 2,500 tons (2,250 t), and the pushing
cylinder is able to exert 1,800 tons (1,620 t) of pressure.
These amazing forces are achieved by using oil pressure.

How Does Radar Tell the Location of an Airplane?

ANSWER A radar system sends invisible signals called radio waves into the air. When the waves touch an airplane they bounce back. The signals return to the antenna of the radar system. By measuring them the system can tell us exactly where the airplane is.

▲ An airport's radar antenna turns.

▲ **Flight control.** A screen shows where the plane is.

Radio wave

Different types of radar units are used in different places

Radar does more than just show where an airplane is located. It is also used to find boats and to show where clouds in hurricanes or typhoons are located. Weather observation radar is usually placed on high hills, but it can also be put on boats and in planes.

▲ Many weather observatories are on hills.

▲ **The radar is in the dome.**

▲ **A weather ship.** The radar is in the dome.

● **To the Parent**

Radar uses microwaves, a type of radio wave which travels in a straight line and at a constant speed, to locate airplanes, boats and other objects. A radar system consists of an antenna, a transmitter, a receiver and an indicator. The indicator is usually a cathode-ray tube and is known as a radar screen. Waves emitted by the antenna are reflected back to it when they contact something. Radar determines an object's location by correlating the direction in which the antenna is pointed and the time it takes the waves to return. Charts can be used with ships' radar screens and those used for weather observation.

How Does a Weather Satellite Stay in One Place Above the Earth?

ANSWER To help keep track of the weather, people send special satellites into space. They fly above the earth's equator. The satellites fly just as fast as the earth is turning, so they stay in the exact same spot in the sky. Even though they are not flying very fast, weather satellites do not appear to us to be moving at all.

■ **Stationary satellite system**

Stationary satellites are placed in orbit above the equator, and they move through space at the same speed at which the earth turns.

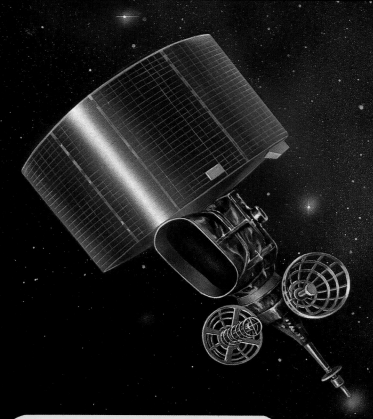

● **To the Parent**

Weather satellites are placed in orbit 22,300 miles (35,680 km) above the equator. They fly through space from west to east at the same speed at which the earth rotates, so if they were visible from the earth they would seem to be standing still. To maintain attitude stability, the satellites turn at about 100 revolutions a minute. Using a camera called a reflectometer, they observe clouds, temperature of sea water and various other factors that influence the weather. Weather satellites have solar batteries, which provide them with power.

Exactly What Does a Weather Satellite Do?

A weather satellite watches the distribution, height and movement of clouds, the temperature of sea water, and other things that affect the weather. It sends this information to the weather bureau as radio signals. A weather satellite also collects weather information from robot buoys drifting on the sea and from ships and sends it back to earth.

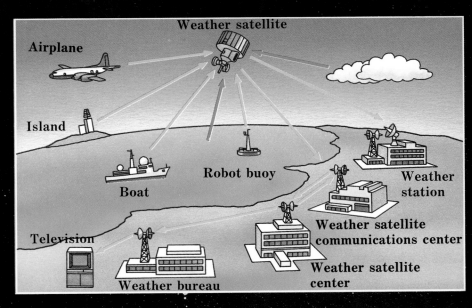

Weather satellite

Airplane

Island

Boat

Robot buoy

Weather station

Weather satellite communications center

Television

Weather bureau

Weather satellite center

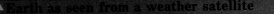

▲ Earth as seen from a weather satellite

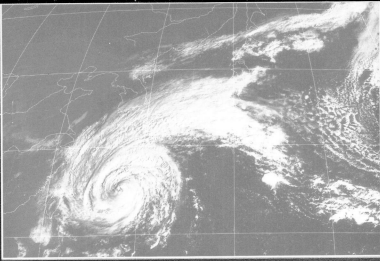

▲ A hurricane photographed by a satellite

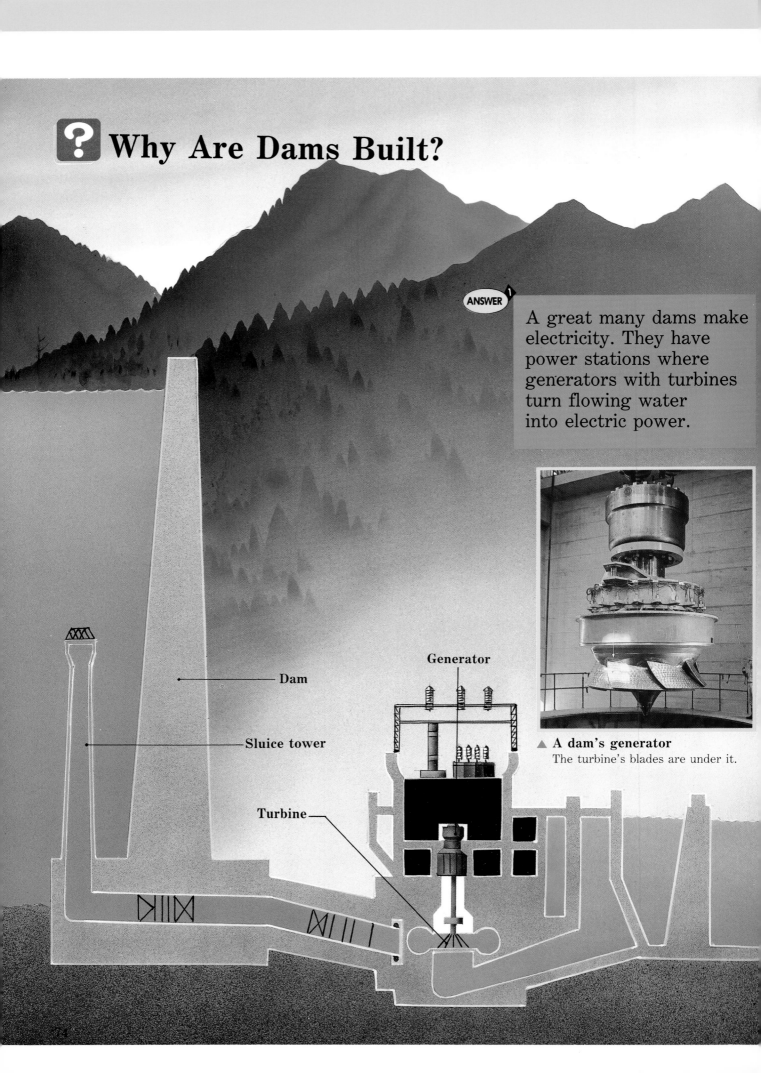

❓ Why Are Dams Built?

ANSWER 1

A great many dams make electricity. They have power stations where generators with turbines turn flowing water into electric power.

Dam

Sluice tower

Generator

Turbine

▲ A dam's generator
The turbine's blades are under it.

ANSWER ② Dams are also built to prevent floods. If there is a heavy rainfall in the mountains, a town downstream on a river that receives the rain may be flooded. To prevent that, a dam is built on the river to hold back the water and release it a little at a time.

ANSWER ③ Dams are also used to store drinking water and water that will be used on farms. The water is stored behind the dam in a lake called a reservoir. If a large amount of water is stored in a dam's reservoir it can prevent a water shortage during dry spells. It lets us use water as we need it.

To the Parent

A dam is a barrier that holds back flowing water. There are flood-control dams (also used to prevent landslides), hydroelectric power dams, irrigation dams and water-supply dams. Some dams may combine all of these purposes. Hydroelectric dams use the force of falling water to turn their turbines, so they are high.

How Do Scientists Measure The Size of an Earthquake?

ANSWER They use a machine called a seismograph. It has a pen that touches a roll of paper. In an earthquake the paper shakes. A weight holds the pen still. The mark on the paper shows the size of the earthquake.

■ A horizontal-motion seismograph

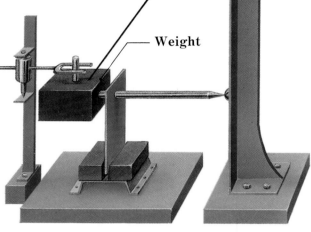

Paper — Pen — Weight

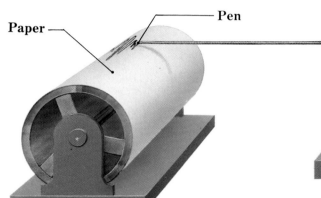

Principle of the seismograph

An earthquake's shock makes things standing on the ground move a lot. Things hanging in the air don't move as much. The hanging weight in a seismograph hardly moves at all.

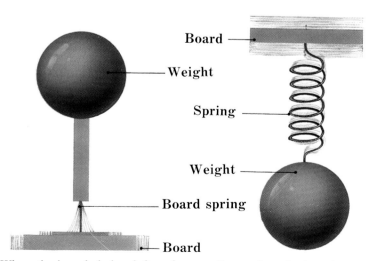

Board
Weight
Spring
Weight
Board spring
Board

When the board shakes left and right the weight does not move.

Even when the board moves up and down the weight does not move.

TRY THIS

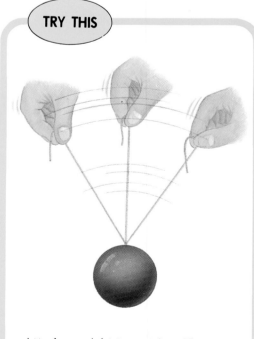

Attach a weight to a string. Then move the string back and forth very quickly. You will see that the weight stays in one place. It does not move the same way that the string does.

How an Earthquake's Movement Travels

The place where an earthquake happens is called the seismic center. The point on the ground above the seismic center is called the epicenter. The shaking caused by the earthquake spreads at a constant speed and becomes weaker as the distance from the seismic center increases.

 MINI-DATA

If there is an earthquake, do not panic and rush outside. It is important to stay calm and crawl under a desk or a table.

● **To the Parent**

When a seismograph equipped with a hanging weight and a drum shakes due to an earthquake the weight does not move. This is because of the law of inertia, which states that an object that is not moving tends to remain in that condition. A seismograph usually consists of two units to record horizontal motion as east-west motion and north-south motion, and one unit to record vertical motion. A magnetic seismograph has recently been developed. Earthquakes produce vertical waves and horizontal waves, with the vertical waves traveling faster than the horizontal ones. That is why when there is an earthquake a small shock is felt first, followed by a bigger shock.

? What Are These Things?

■ Tanker

A tanker is a ship that carries a liquid cargo. It has large tanks inside, which is why it's called a tanker. Oil is one of the things that's transported in a tanker.

An oil tanker is huge, isn't it! It can carry lots of oil.

■ Blimp

G-SKSE

A blimp is an aircraft that's filled with a gas called helium. Because it's lighter than air, it can fly. And because it has a propeller and an engine, a blimp can move through the air by itself.

■ Lighthouse

A lighthouse is a tall building found near the seashore. At night its bright light shines through a big lens. Ships can tell where they are by the lighthouse, which is visible from far away.

■ Dam

One reason dams are built is to generate electricity. As water flows through this dam, electricity is produced by the generators inside. Dams also prevent floods. Behind this dam a huge lake has backed up.

■ Gas storage tanks

These tanks store the gas that we use for cooking and heating. At night and in the summer less gas is used, so the extra is stored here. Factories also use some of the gas, which is under pressure in the tanks.

■ High-voltage power lines

Every day we use electricity that's been produced at an electric power plant. The electricity comes from the generating plant on high-power transmission lines like the ones shown here. After the electricity is cut down to a lower level of power, it comes into our homes on smaller lines so that we can use it as we need it.

● **To the Parent**

Tankers for oil are called dirty tankers, while those for gasoline are called clean tankers. Blimps today use only helium, an inert gas. Lighthouses are classified by the size of their lenses, not the power of their lamps. Dams have been used to generate electricity only since about 1900. Gas tanks store mixtures of manufactured gases. A high-power line carries about 3,000 volts of electricity.

❓ And What Are These?

■ Radio telescope

A radio telescope picks up electric waves coming from space. These telescopes are used to track spaceships and satellites that are orbiting the earth.

■ Space shuttle

A space shuttle is something like a bus that carries people back and forth between the earth and space. On board the space shuttle scientists can do experiments and make observations in space. The shuttle can also be used to carry satellites into space where they can be launched easily.

■ Sundial

As long as the sun is out a sundial can be used for telling time. The sundial's shadow moves and shows what hour it is as the position of the sun changes in the sky. Long before the clock was invented people used shadows of trees or rocks to tell what time it was. Those were the first, simple sundials.

● **To the Parent**

A radio telescope usually has parabolic antennas, the surfaces of which are very thin metal sheets or thin metal nets. A space shuttle can be used repeatedly and can serve as a laboratory in space, where scientists carry out experiments. Shadows were used for telling time as long ago as 3500 B.C. The oldest sundial known today was made in Egypt in about the 8th Century B.C.

Growing-Up Album

How Do They Work?

Here are five machines that are often found around the house. Can you find each of them in the picture on the right? What is needed to make each thing work? Who uses these different machines in your family?

What Do They Do?

All the machines and equipment that you see
in this city have a special job to do.

■ Think about it

Look at these six machines
or pieces of equipment on
the right. Each one has a
special purpose in the life
of the city. Think about it
carefully and decide what
these things do. Which ones
have you used? Which ones
have done some work for you?

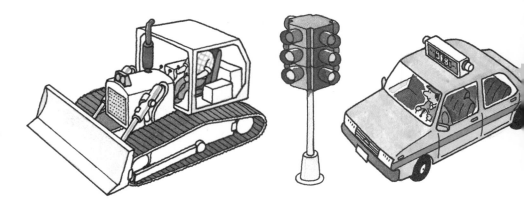

Where Do They Get Their Power?

All of these things need power to
make them work. As you know now,
there are several kinds of power.

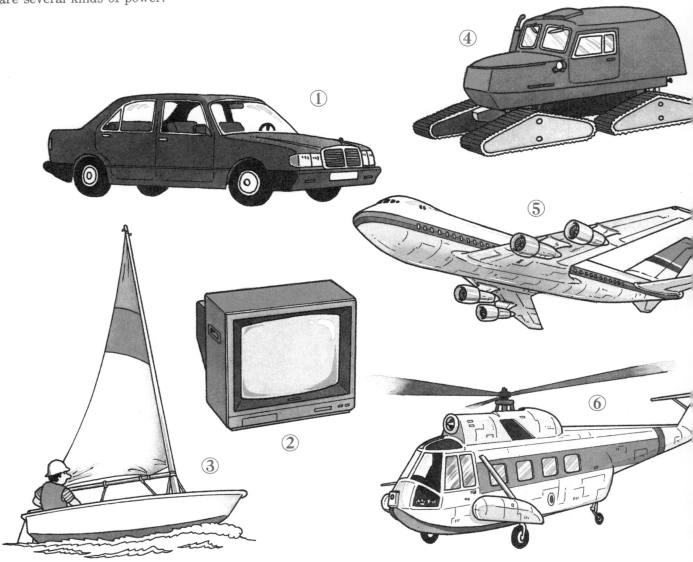

■ Think about it

The things you see in the
picture above all use some kind
of power. At the right you see
pictures that will remind you of
five kinds of power. Think about
it and decide what kind of power
makes each of those things work.

Oil and gasoline   **Electricity**

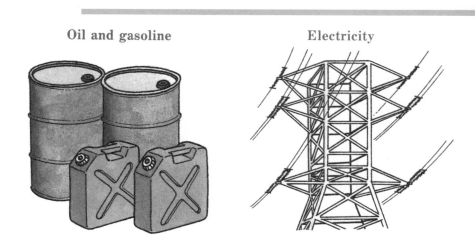

Batteries

Sunlight and heat

Wind

Oil: 1, 4, 5, 6, 14   Electricity: 2, 7, 9   Battery: 10, 13
Sunlight: 8, 12   Wind: 3, 11

A Child's First Library of Learning

How Things Work

Time-Life Books Inc. is a wholly owned subsidiary of
Time Incorporated.
Time-Life Books, Alexandria, Virginia
Children's Publishing

Director:	Robert H. Smith
Associate Director:	R. S. Wotkyns III
Editorial Director:	Neil Kagan
Promotion Director:	Kathleen Tresnak
Editorial Consultants:	Jacqueline A. Ball
	Andrew Gutelle

Editorial Supervision by:
International Editorial Services Inc.
Tokyo, Japan

Editor:	C. E. Berry
Editorial Research:	Miki Ishii
Design:	Kim Bolitho
Writer:	Pauline Bush
Educational Consultants:	Janette Bryden
	Laurie Hanawa
Translation:	Ronald K. Jones
Cover Photo:	Craig Aurness©/
	Woodfin Camp, Inc.

TIME
LIFE ®

Library of Congress Cataloging in Publication Data
How things work.
    p.   cm. — (A Child's first library of learning)
    Summary: Questions and answers provide information
about how cameras, elevators, car engines, tops, yo-yos,
and other devices work. Includes charts, diagrams, and an
activities section.
    ISBN 0-8094-4873-4.   ISBN 0-8094-4874-2 (lib. bdg.)
    1. Technology—Juvenile literature.   [1. Technology—
Miscellanea.   2. Questions and answers.]   I. Time-Life
Books.   II. Series.
T48.H74 1989   620—dc20   89-4535
©1989 Time-Life Books Inc.
©1983 Gakken Co. Ltd.
All rights reserved. No part of this book may be reproduced in
any form or by any electronic or mechanical means, including
information storage and retrieval devices or systems, without
prior written permission from the publisher, except that brief
passages may be quoted for review.

Fifth printing 1993. Printed in U.S.A.
Published simultaneously in Canada.

TIME-LIFE is a trademark of Time Warner Inc. U.S.A.